INJURY, REHABILITATION AND INSURANCE

Injury, Rehabilitation and Insurance:
My Struggle for Survival

by

Molly Davison

The Pentland Press Limited
Edinburgh · Cambridge · Durham · USA

© Molly Davison 2000

First published in 2000 by
The Pentland Press Ltd.
1 Hutton Close
South Church
Bishop Auckland
Durham

All rights reserved.
Unauthorised duplication
contravenes existing laws.

British Library Cataloguing in Publication Data.
A catalogue record for this book is available
from the British Library.

ISBN 1 85821 753 9

Typeset by George Wishart & Associates, Whitley Bay.
Printed and bound by Antony Rowe Ltd., Chippenham.

*To Fred, my husband
and
to all the staff at the five hospitals
where I received treatment*

Contents

List of Illustrations ix

Chapter I	September-November 1991	1
Chapter II	17 December 1993	5
Chapter III	December 1993-January 1994	10
Chapter IV	January-March 1994	18
Chapter V	The Rehabilitation Unit	30
Chapter VI	December 1994-December 1995	41
Chapter VII	January-February 1996	48
Chapter VIII	March-April 1996	53
Chapter IX	May-June 1996	59
Chapter X	July-December 1996	67
Chapter XI	January-February 1997	98
Chapter XII	March-April 1997	101
Chapter XIII	May-October 1997	105
Chapter XIV	November 1997-January 1998	117
Chapter XV	13 Crucial Days	125
Chapter XVI	April 1998-March 1999	144

List of Illustrations

Home!	3
One item of Fred's DIY coma management kit	21
The bungalow	45
Ground floor plan of the bungalow	46
The proposed ground floor plan showing the position of the screen	60
Underpinning the foundations	63
Laying the new foundations	64
Progress?	68
And it grew and grew	70
More progress and some light gardening	72
Looking down on the collapsed ceiling	75
Building the ramped path	77
The 'old' kitchen	86

CHAPTER I

September-November 1991

This is a personal view of the events surrounding and following a serious car accident, an accident that brought about my complete metamorphosis. To bring about this change I had to learn many things about myself, other people, the health, caring and legal professions. The learning was always difficult, often painful, but certainly essential. Maybe the recording of my experiences will make it easier for others who have to follow a similar path, or guide those who try to help them. I have only recorded the events and my response to them. I leave analysis to the reader.

To begin with some details. I was born in 1945. My interests are reflected by my qualifications. I think it is fair to conclude that the acquisition of these qualifications played a large part in shaping my personality. I completed my full-time education at Durham University. The results of years of study equipped me with a BSc and a Diploma in Education; I was a Fellow of the Institute of Swimming Teachers and a Licentiate of the London College of Music. Twenty years later I added an Advanced Diploma in Education to my qualifications and for a time I was a teacher tutor with the Department of Education at Cambridge University.

I had a varied teaching experience which included posts in the state and independent sectors. With a break of eight years to have a family, I slowly mounted the education ladder. At the time of the accident I was a senior teacher, Head of Science and the Coordinator for Science and Technology in an 11-18

INJURY, REHABILITATION AND INSURANCE

comprehensive school. I had one other break from teaching, in addition to the break to have a family. I spent a year as a County Evaluator for a Records of Achievement project. Over the years I acquired lecturing and external examining experience. I was very involved with teacher training for the introduction of Records of Achievement, Balanced Science and the use of Information Technology across the curriculum. I represented teachers on a County Steering Committee for Records of Achievement and on the Biology Subject Committee for the University of Cambridge Local Examinations Syndicate.

On a more personal theme I am married with two children, Kathryn and Matthew. Over the years I developed a love of cooking and sewing. We have lived in several houses, of necessity garden design and gardening were added to my interests. My husband, Fred, was relocated to Berkshire before my children had completed their secondary education, so the family had only lived in the area for a few years when the accident occurred. Fred had lived and worked in Berkshire for three years longer than me.

Relocation for the family was anything but straightforward. Fortunately, my children were at university. The building of our new house was not completed for the beginning of the autumn term. I began teaching at my new school whilst living in a thatched, holiday cottage in Mapledurham. All my books and belongings remained in Cambridgeshire.

The agreed date for the move arrived, because over the years we had acquired a lot of possessions and as the move was from Cambridgeshire to Berkshire, it required two days. We arrived to a very odd scene: a very large removal van was parked in the road; an assortment of puzzled builders and removal men were standing around a bonfire outside a house with a steep sandy track as an approach. On closer inspection, we discovered an equally puzzled plumber wandering around upstairs with a bath.

All too soon it became clearer – the developer's promise of

SEPTEMBER-NOVEMBER 1991

Home!

completion by the agreed date had been empty. He did not have the men or the means to complete the fixtures and fittings in time. We decided on a plan of action, or to be truthful we had no other option – we could only go back to Mapledurham for a few more days before the cottage was rented to someone else, the removal van was needed back in Cambridgeshire. The sale of our old house was complete. We had nowhere, other than the unfinished house, to store our belongings and nowhere to live.

The plan involved cleaning out the double garage, providing more fuel for the bonfire. This operation allowed space to store the boxes which were stacked from the floor to the rafters several rows deep. We lived amongst the stored furniture in the unfinished house. It wasn't that we couldn't find anything, we knew exactly where it was – in a box in the garage – but we couldn't get at it!

Very shortly afterwards this phase ended and the true situation became clear: the developer went bankrupt and the National

House Builders Corporation became involved. The house was finished by a local builder, who completed the work around us. Knowledge of a very good local builder, who was prepared to work in difficult circumstances, was to prove invaluable several years later.

CHAPTER II

17 December 1993

The end of the Autumn term and Christmas were almost upon me. The term had been particularly difficult, different and exciting. The school had a new head teacher and the staff and governors had decided to transform the school into a City Technology College. I was deeply involved with the planning for this initiative and I was running an after-school, Information Technology course for the staff. I had enjoyed a very busy week. I had taken my tutor group on an evening trip to the ice-skating rink, run the course and I had attended a Christmas dinner with staff from Fred's work. By the end of the week I was almost on my knees but I had promised to go to dinner with a group of friends at St Ives.

After a day's teaching I travelled by rail to Huntingdon, Cambridgeshire. Apparently, the last things I said to Fred included a reminder for him to meet me off the train, at the end of my return journey the following day as we needed to go Christmas shopping. Fred had taken a day's annual leave to bring Kathryn home from Bristol University, while Matthew was already down from Nottingham University and planned to spend the evening with his girlfriend, attending a departmental Christmas party held at the Research Institute where Fred worked. Both Kathryn and Matthew had examinations after the Christmas holidays but they had decided to enjoy the Christmas period before beginning some hard work.

INJURY, REHABILITATION AND INSURANCE

Things went as planned until the early evening: Matthew went to his party; Fred and Kathryn returned home and were enjoying an evening meal; I was almost at St Ives. Then plans and events started to deviate.

I was collected from the railway station by my friend's son, who was driving a Metro car. We were almost at my friend's house when we were involved in a serious accident. After conducting skid tests the accident inspector's report came to the following conclusion:

> The Metro approached the junction round the long flowing, right hand bend at a speed which was in excess of the safe maximum speed.
>
> Alternatively, the Metro was travelling below the safe approach speed but the driver was not paying the proper amount of attention to his driving and did not see the car waiting to turn.
>
> Whichever of the two possibilities is correct we do know that, at some point, the driver saw a stationary car opposite the mouth of the junction but was travelling too fast to be able to stop behind it. He turned the steering wheel to the right and braked so hard that the car began to skid and rotate in a clockwise direction. The Metro crossed the central line directly into the path of an approaching Subaru Estate car. The front of the heavy Subaru struck the Metro in the vicinity of the passenger door with the momentum of the much lighter Metro being sufficient to cause the Subaru to stop on impact and causing the mud from its wheel arches to fall to the ground.

I fortunately cannot recall the accident. The driver pleaded guilty to careless driving.

Apparently I was cut free from the car and received attention at the scene from paramedics. I was then taken to Addenbrookes Hospital in Cambridge. The driver was suffering from shock but was not seriously injured; he was taken to the local hospital for a check-up. Later the police went to inform my friend who telephoned Fred.

17 DECEMBER 1993

Fred and Kathryn's meal was disturbed by the telephone call. They initially thought it was a call to say I had arrived safely. It was not. A very tearful and distressed friend briefly told Fred what had happened, how serious it was and where I had been taken. The policeman then took the telephone and gave more details; he expressed his concern about Fred driving from Reading to Cambridge. Fred assured him he would be all right and rang Addenbrookes Hospital to confirm the story. Before leaving he rang a senior member of staff at the Research Institute to get a message to Matthew.

Matthew and his girlfriend Jay immediately left the party and decided they would also drive to Cambridge. They had to be driven to Jay's home to collect her car, then they also began the long journey to Cambridge.

Fred's journey to Cambridge began at a local garage, the first of two fortuitous events. He met a colleague of mine and told him where he was going and why. My colleague informed my headmaster, who was then able to make arrangements for my absence and explain to the children what had happened.

The long journey began. As the miles fled past the seriousness of the whole incident began to dawn on Fred and Kathryn. Each was silently preoccupied with their own thoughts. Kathryn remembered the shudder she had while watching Alistair Cook's 1993 New Year programme. Had this been an omen?

Fred and Kathryn were the first to arrive at the Accident and Emergency unit at Addenbrookes Hospital. It was here that primary resuscitation and identification of the injuries took place. They could not be seen immediately and were shown to a side room. Later they were joined by Matthew and Jay. A junior doctor came to explain the seriousness of the situation and was later joined by the consultant. She touched Fred on the shoulder and told him it was 'touch and go'.

The doctors had decided to send me to Papworth Hospital. Fred

INJURY, REHABILITATION AND INSURANCE

saw me for the first time as I was about to leave. He and each member of the family were allowed momentarily to go into the ambulance.

It was now that the second fortuitous event had its effect. Papworth Hospital is less than ten miles from Addenbrookes Hospital. With its sophisticated facilities for heart surgery, it had the necessary equipment for one of my injuries, a transection of the major blood vessel from the heart. When an intensive care bed became available I was returned to Addenbrookes Hospital, however there was continued blood loss during the following twelve hours which led to an emergency abdominal operation. During the operation it was found there was a tear in the upper part of my spleen: I was bleeding profusely necessitating a splenectomy. The orthopaedic injuries also required treatment, I was given a left dynamic hip screw fixation and my broken left femur was plated. My liver was torn, my left cheek bone broken, my left eye damaged and I had extensive bruising.

The next few weeks were chaotic for the family as I remained in a coma in Cambridge; our home was in Berkshire. No-one knew what was going to happen next or if I would survive.

This section is only to be read by those of you who have an interest in detail. It gives more information about the operations and can be omitted by those readers who do not require such knowledge.

After immediate resuscitation I underwent a CT scan of the head and abdomen. The initial CT scan of the head was normal, the CT scan of the abdomen revealed intra-abdominal free blood and a tear of the liver. I was injected with a dye to study the great blood vessels. This identified a contained bleed and tearing of the aorta at its junction between the arch and descending aorta distal to the left subclavian branch. Therefore there was a tear in a major blood vessel from the heart.

My left femur was fractured and was placed under traction. I was

17 DECEMBER 1993

transferred to the cardio-thoracic surgery unit at Papworth Hospital. The aortic transection was repaired by cross-clamping the aorta between the carotid and the left subclavian branches, the torn section was resected and a primary anastomosis performed. This was achieved in fifteen minutes. The abdomen was drained of blood. I remained in a coma and was returned to Addenbrookes Hospital.

The abdominal bleeding continued. An emergency operation identified profuse bleeding from the spleen. The spleen was removed. The left hip was stabilized with a dynamic hip screw.

Ventilation support was withdrawn and an assessment on 6 January indicated I was still in a coma, making no eye opening or verbal responses and localizing to painful stimuli only.

The CT scan was repeated and showed evidence of diffuse ischaemic changes throughout the brain and bleeding from the brain stem consistent with the traumatic injury.

CHAPTER III

December 1993-January 1994

The previous chapter recounts the essential features of the operations; my family had to live through this experience and its immediate effects. I am only able to record the events I was told about and, like you, must use imagination to fill the gaps.

When the operation in Papworth Hospital was completed I was placed in the intensive care unit to await transfer back to Addenbrookes Hospital. After the first part of the operation the surgeon left the operating theatre to talk with Fred, still wearing his bloodstained operating theatre boots. He was able to tell Fred that after the first part of the operation all was going well but further exploratory surgery was needed to investigate bleeding in the abdomen. My family obviously needed somewhere to stay. It was the early hours of the morning and a nurse suggested the nearby Papworth Motel. Luckily there had been a Christmas party and the staff were still on duty. Two double rooms were free and they were able to provide the necessary accommodation.

18 December
My family made arrangements to stay at the motel until it closed for the Christmas week. Because of the proximity of Christmas only very close friends and the immediate family were informed of the accident.

The next day my family visited Papworth Hospital; I was returned to Addenbrookes Hospital as soon as an intensive care bed was available. They watched the ambulance leave and followed it to Addenbrookes Hospital.

For the rest of that day, they sat in a small waiting room with members of other patients' families – all were in the same worried state – and returned to the motel at about 10.30 p.m. As Fred was going to bed there was a telephone call asking for permission to carry out surgery on my fractured leg and hip. The doctor explained that it was not unusual to do surgery during the night – there are about fourteen operating theatres which work night and day. Fred gave verbal permission for the operation.

19 December
First thing in the morning Fred rang the hospital. The staff nurse explained that on moving me to theatre they discovered that the spleen was still bleeding and it was decided to carry out a splenectomy before the hip surgery; I was stable but still in a coma.

The family had breakfast and set off for the hospital. Fred was told he could stay by the bed in the intensive care unit, ICU, and would only be sent out when the nurse needed to carry out some medical procedure.

I was on a ventilator, life-support machine, and regularly turned from side to side to try to prevent muscle spasm. I was the recipient of so much blood, Fred has become a regular blood donor! When visitors sat on my left side I was so bruised and swollen I was hardly recognisable. Matthew and Jay drove back to Reading to collect more clothes, cancel the papers, and inform the neighbours and the Research Institute of the events. The day wore on, so Kathryn and Fred took breaks by going to the hospital cafeteria. It was Christmas week, the decorations were up and the tree lights continually chimed carols. They returned to the motel that night.

20 December
There was no change in my condition and my family was unable to

INJURY, REHABILITATION AND INSURANCE

get any firm information, however, the head of the ICU spoke to Fred and said he was going to arrange for a second CT scan (brain scan) and would then be in a better position to advise on my condition and prospects. Matthew and Jay had returned from Reading and broke up the day by going out for walks to get away from the intense atmosphere of the hospital waiting room. Jay bought Kathryn a miniature tapestry kit to keep her mind occupied.

The nurses offered the family the opportunity to stay in amenity beds, which were spare hospital beds or nurses' beds. This arrangement meant they could stay nearby and visit the ICU late at night and early in the morning, although the rooms were not comfortable and none of them got much sleep. Matthew and Fred shared a nurse's room in the tower block, but there was only a single bed, so Fred slept on a mattress on the floor.

21 December
Kathleen, my sister, travelled down from Yorkshire. The CT scan was carried out and the doctor in charge ordered withdrawal of the morphine to see if I could be aroused from the coma. The day wore on and they were all very tense. They stayed in the amenity beds. Kathleen joined Kathryn and Jay in their room, but none of them slept much.

Fred got up at 7.00 a.m. and went to the ICU. The nurses had already turned off the life-support machine, I was breathing on my own but had not come out of the coma.

The doctor would not talk to the family until he had a copy of the written report from the neurosurgeon. Eventually, just before lunch, he saw Kathryn, Matthew and Fred. The prognosis was not good, the brain scan showed up haemorrhage, oedema and swelling of the brain stem. He did not hold out much hope. He said they would now take me out of intensive care and move me to a side ward, where I would be cared for but it did not look as though I would recover. They were devastated but thanked him and his staff for what they had done. When Fred returned to the ICU and told the nurse I would wish my organs to be donated, she seemed surprised by the gloomy prognosis and said it might not necessarily come to that.

My family talked and decided they could do no more for me. They were all exhausted, it was two days before Christmas day and they were again running out of clean clothes. They decided to go home, my family to Reading, Kathleen to Yorkshire; they all travelled home late in the evening, Matthew driving our car and Jay driving Kathryn. Fred fully expected to be arranging a funeral and Matthew and he talked about having it in Cambridge.

23 December
In the morning Fred rang the hospital, they washed their clothes and went shopping for food. Later that day the ward sister telephoned and said they had moved me to the neurosurgical ward and the neurosurgeon wished to speak to Fred. He made an appointment for 10.00 a.m. the following day.

24 December
Matthew and Fred travelled to Cambridge by train. Jay took them to the station for the 07.31 to Paddington. On the way to the station they were stopped by the police who were checking drivers and breathalysing. Kathryn felt unable to cope with a return visit to Cambridge and wanted time to collect her thoughts. She stayed at home, spending some time with Jay.

On arrival at Cambridge Matthew and Fred discovered I had been moved into a high dependency unit, the Annex of the Neurosurgery Department. After visiting the unit, a very claustrophobic and depressing place, they stood in the corridor for about forty-five minutes awaiting the interview with the consultant.

They eventually met the neurosurgeon who informed them I

was developing pneumonia and he wished to know if, and how, they wished to have me treated. The interview was a bizarre affair held in a room recently vacated by Christmas revellers. The staff nurse in attendance had to stand with her heel against the door to prevent junior staff from entering to raid the last of the mince pies and other Christmas fare.

They were informed that my chances of survival were very poor and that, if I did survive, I would be seriously disabled, possibly with severe brain damage and therefore unable to lead a fulfilling life. The situation would be likely to cause me great frustration if I were to survive and could think.

They tentatively agreed the ground rules, subject to discussion with Kathryn and Kathleen – I was to be treated with powerful antibiotics by the intravenous route; if my breathing stopped I was not to be resuscitated.

Fred and Matthew went into Cambridge to buy Kathryn her Christmas present – two volumes of a veterinary surgery manual – bought some other Christmas presents and then went back to the railway station. They travelled on the last train to London on Christmas Eve. On the platform Matthew said, 'What a Christmas present to be asked if I want my mother to be given life-saving treatment.'

Kathryn, Kathleen and Jay agreed with what had been said to the neurosurgeon. Kathryn, with her knowledge of surgery, considered that if I stopped breathing for any reason then resuscitation would only be temporary and it would inevitably happen again.

25 December
Jay cooked a turkey and they spent a miserable Christmas day.

26 December
Kathryn, Matthew and Fred returned to Cambridge by car while

DECEMBER 1993–JANUARY 1994

Jay went to stay with her parents. When they arrived they were told I had pneumonia and the doctor had already begun pumping in strong antibiotics by the intravenous route. They were regularly asked to leave the bedside so the nursing staff could clear my airways using a suction device.

The family returned to Reading. On telephoning the hospital Fred was told that things looked more serious and I was exhibiting Chain Stokes respiration, a sign that I may not survive for long. Kathryn was not convinced by what the nurse described as she had seen animals exhibiting Chain Stokes respiration. The family were intending to go back the next day anyway.

27-29 December

Early the next day they returned to the hospital with clothes ready to stay for some time. Fred asked about accommodation and was told there were rooms at a hostel in the hospital grounds for families of long-stay patients; they could not face the amenity beds again. The rooms were comfortable and provided with a kettle and a television – it meant there was somewhere comfortable and quiet to come to after sitting in the unit. Matthew and Fred shared a double bed; Kathryn stayed on her own. My condition did not improve. They continued eating in the staff canteen or cafeteria and spending time in the unit or going into Cambridge for a break before they returned home on the evening of 30 December.

1-2 January

They visited again. Kathleen joined them on the 2nd. I was moved to a separate room. For the first time Fred thought I was responding to requests to squeeze his hand. He told the senior staff nurse who was looking after me but he did not believe Fred. He said that it was likely to be a reflex response and probably meant little. He went off duty and they did not see him for some time.

When they did see him later, he told them that as he had got me

INJURY, REHABILITATION AND INSURANCE

to wriggle my toes, on request, I could be beginning to come round. Both Kathryn and Matthew needed to prepare for examinations and they all returned home on the evening of 2 January.

3 January
The family stayed at home for the New Year Bank Holiday.

4 January
Fred felt unable to go into work. Matthew started his revision and Kathryn went to her foster practice. All veterinary students have to spend time with a practice before they can qualify. Foster practices are chosen by the university at a location near the student's home – Kathryn's was near Newbury so she went there to take her mind off things.

5 January
Fred went into work, but asked a colleague to tell people not to stop him to enquire what had happened; he avoided using the staff canteen.

6 January
Fred took the train to Cambridge. He met one of the doctors he had seen on Christmas Eve and spoke to him about my response to simple requests. The doctor concluded it was highly unlikely.

The hospital staff told Fred they were trying to arrange to have me moved to Reading. I would be moving between hospital trusts, therefore there could be a delay while arrangements were made and while they sorted out who was paying for the transfer.

8-9 January
Matthew, Jay, Kathryn and Fred set off for Cambridge by car. Jay especially asked to go as she had not seen me since I was in the

DECEMBER 1993-JANUARY 1994

ICU. The roads were very icy and it had been snowing during the previous week. There was a lot of snow lying in the fields and on the roadsides in Bedfordshire and South Cambridgeshire.

I was still in a room of my own. Fred stayed over until 9 January but the others returned home. He travelled home by train on the Sunday evening.

11 January
Matthew told Fred he felt unable to face all the well-meaning questions and sympathy from his university friends. Fred wrote a letter to his tutor to explain the situation and Matthew drove Fred to Nottingham for the start of his term.

Fred drove on to Cambridge. The hospital staff told Fred I would be moved to Reading as soon as an ambulance could be arranged.

12 January
Fred had a 9.00 a.m. appointment with a firm of solicitors. During the interview the solicitor had a trainee sitting in with him. They were both astounded by Fred's story. The solicitor suggested that they should arrange, through the Court of Protection, for Fred to take charge of my affairs. This arrangement would allow a claim for damages to be started. The solicitor said he would write to the defendant and tell him we were going to claim damages and ask him for the name of his insurers.

Later that day there was a phone call from the hospital to say that I was to be moved on 13 January. Jay said she would come over and stay the night to drive Kathryn to her foster practice while Fred took the train to Cambridge to travel in the ambulance with me.

CHAPTER IV

January-March 1994

13 January

The ambulance journey to Reading was arranged for the afternoon. While Fred was waiting, he spoke to a friend who had been coming to see me regularly. She had realized there would be some days when I had no visitors and she did not like the thought of me being on my own each day.

We left at last and the stay in the second hospital came to an end. I had survived one more stage – each stage was to bring additional changes, different requirements from the medical staff and difficult demands on anybody that became involved. I was moving nearer home but I was still in a coma and Fred had no reliable indication as to whether I would remain in the coma, or for how long; if I did come out of the coma, he had no way of knowing what would emerge. I, like you, can only imagine the difficulties this state of affairs caused for everyone, but especially for him.

I was told the long journey to Reading was not very comfortable, one member of the ambulance crew repeatedly asked Fred about the accident. Fred had read that you should not discuss details of injuries within the hearing of patients who are in a coma (some people have recovered and can remember what they heard). He was sure I knew something was going on because I gripped his hand throughout the whole journey, but he need not have worried, I cannot recall the journey.

JANUARY-MARCH 1994

We entered the Reading hospital via the Accident and Emergency unit and I was admitted to an orthopaedic ward. The staff nurse told Fred, although this ward was primarily an orthopaedic ward, they had experience with the care of head injury patients. He was very confident about me improving. 'This one's a fighter, she will survive.'

The first ray of hope. Fred had to leave the hospital, collect the car and drive to Kathryn's foster practice to bring her back to Reading. They both returned to the hospital to talk to the staff nurse and the Medical Registrar.

14-17 January

A new phase was beginning, which required responses from everybody who was personally involved with me and whose lifestyles prior to Christmas 1993 did not fit comfortably with the present situation.

Matthew had been the first of my children to face this dilemma, while Kathryn felt she was letting me down going back to university. Fred assured her that I would want her to continue with her veterinary training, but considered he ought to be with me. Colleagues and the staff at the hospital wisely advised him to carry on with his job. He visited every morning before going to work and every evening after work. A telephone tree was established to widen the circle of people who were aware of the accident and for those people that wanted to be kept informed. Fred bought an answerphone, so that his daily routine was not dictated by the innumerable telephone calls. He spent much of the weekends with me.

Kathryn, Matthew and Kathleen visited every other weekend. My other visitors included colleagues from school, where supply arrangements had been arranged to cover what was obviously going to be a long absence.

I was facing, but unaware of, a different set of medical problems.

INJURY, REHABILITATION AND INSURANCE

The nasal gastric tube, which despite my comatose condition I had persistently removed, was replaced by a gastrostomy tube. This tube pierced my abdominal wall and allowed food, liquids and all the medication to go directly into my stomach. The remaining problems did not enjoy such a simple resolution as the spasticity continued to develop and I remained in a coma.

At the hospital a diary recording my progress was begun. Entries were made by the nurses, therapists, visitors, family and friends (see pp. 22-3). Much later, I began to complete a page-a-day diary. These diaries, the various experts' reports and all the legal documentation have enabled me to write this book.

I always imagined being in a coma was like being asleep – certainly television programmes had given me this impression. My husband was equally ill-informed. When I was in hospital in Cambridge, Fred bought several books describing the management of a coma, and he began to put into practice what he read. He made a notice that was placed above my bed, requesting all visitors to assume I could hear, therefore all conversations had to be positive; strong smells and touch were other senses that were considered important. Kathryn made a 'feely' board of materials of different textures e.g. anaglypta, velvet, sandpaper etc. and Fred bought a selection of aromatic liquids.

Each day I was lifted out of bed to sit in a chair. I was unable to sit by myself therefore cushions were used to support me. All I could move were my eyes. I could not open my eyelids therefore the movement was detected through the closed lids. I progressed slowly, and within a few days I was able to lift and turn my head allowing my hair to be brushed. I opened my mouth to allow a nurse to clean my teeth. I was soon able to squeeze the nurse's hand to indicate 'yes' when I was ready to go to bed or when I was in pain.

> *Molly* is severely brain-injured.
>
> She is in coma. However, she may be able to see or hear or feel you. Would you please identify yourself to her.
>
> Would you please:
>
> 1. Not say anything which is negative in her presence.
> 2. Not laugh at anything she does.
> 3. Tell her if you are going to touch her.
> 4. Tell her where you are going to touch her.
> 5. Tell her what you are going to do.
> 6. Talk to her as a person.
> 7. Talk to her slowly, in a loud, clear voice.
> 8. If there are more than one of you, do not all talk together.
> 9. Praise her, if you think there has been a response to you.
> 10. Say that she is going to get better, and that you are going to help her.

One item of Fred's DIY coma management kit.

18 January

The physiotherapist indicated I could move my right leg and arm when asked to do so. I had begun to mumble. These were early indications of the level of comprehension I had retained.

20 January

I had a bath and was propped into a chair. I opened both eyes whilst looking down. I could swing my right leg. A day later I was responding to voices and music by moving my right arm and leg. The nursing staff wondered if I would benefit from a massage given by the nurse attached to the ICU. She was an aromatherapist, the hospital had realized the value of the techniques she used with seriously ill patients. This casual observation led to years of invaluable passive massage – the aromatherapist always used to let me smell the oils, reinforcing Fred's ideas concerning revival.

Tues 18th   14:45
Squeezed Hand for "Yes" when asked if wanted to go back to bed.
                         Jackie

Tues. 18th. 17.15.
Molly raised her right arm in the air when I entered the room and said "hello" to her.
Molly also turned towards Glenis when she spoke to her, early afternoon. Heather Cook.

Tuesday 18th pm
Raised her hand again when I told her I was in the room with her –
Seemed to want to open her eyes – moved her right hand to her eyes when I was talking with her – not confirmed

Tuesday 18th Nov
Tried to squeeze my hand with her ® hand when I asked if she was in pain.
                Jayne Hancock

19.1.94 06.00
After turning Molly she opened her ® eye.
When I asked Molly to squeeze my hand if she could open her eyes, she did.

19.1.94   7.00 - 8.00
Molly rubbed her right hand against her right eye a couple of times.
Felt sure she squeezed my hand with her left hand when I asked her - not confirmed

19/1/94. 10.00am
Moving ® arm & leg when asked to stretch them out to prevent contractures. Has also moved head and mumbled in the last few days but not today. Karen (physio).

22 January
I had a high temperature but still responded to simple requests, e.g. raise your thumb, squeeze my hand. I was unable to cough, therefore my chest was beaten regularly by the physiotherapists to keep the airways clear.

23 January
I opened my eyes, turned my head and responded to my name. The following day I opened my eyes and tried to vocalize when the nurse said 'good morning'. Later that day I held out my arm when blood was collected.

25 January
When a nurse mentioned using lip balm, I held out my index finger, she put it in the jar and I tried to rub it into my lower lip.

Over the following days I was supported for longer periods in the chair, further evidence of a mismatch with television programmes, when coma patients are always portrayed laying in bed! Fred told me I watched as people walked around the room and I seemed fascinated by the tag on my left arm.

1 February
My tutor group sent me a large pink bear. I responded to comments from the pupils by several groans. These simple responses gave Fred another indication of the level of comprehension I had retained. I can remember doing this, despite being in a coma!

2 February
A simple method of communication was evolved.
   Thumb up = yes
   Fist = no
   Over the following days I was able to use this communication method with my son, husband, sister and the nurses. I was much

more responsive to simple requests. I took the toothbrush and attempted to clean my teeth. I also brushed my hair, wiped my nose and mouth, used lip balm and helped put on my nightdress by moving my arm when requested.

6 February
Fred used a children's game to demonstrate my ability to distinguish different colours. I was able to pick out the numbers on the dice and can remember doing this!

7 February
Following a painful episode with a urinary catheter, a nurse suggested writing a list of sentences on a communication sheet. If I could still read, I would be able to point to indicate the nature of the problem.

8 February
Following the nurse's suggestion Fred tried to get me to respond to a written instruction. I did not respond but when a nurse asked me to smile, I moved my lips slightly.

10 February
I waved goodbye to Fred when he told me he was leaving for work.

12 February
I gave a spontaneous and distinct thumbs up.

15 February
I used Kathryn's 'feely' board with a nurse. She offered me a choice of magazines; I clearly indicated which one I wanted.

17 February, 7.00 a.m.
Fred came as usual before going to work. He looked into my room

INJURY, REHABILITATION AND INSURANCE

but he did not see me, although the nursing staff assured him I was in the room. I was indeed in the room but I was under the bed surrounded by tubes. The bed's side was broken and held in place by bandage. This temporary solution failed, the bed's side collapsed and I fell out and rolled under the bed. This was a very effective method of revival, but certainly not one advocated in Fred's books!

I thought I was dreaming. I cannot remember being put back into the bed but I can remember playing a game with myself. I would close my eyes and when I opened them I thought everything would be back to normal. I can remember doing this, over what must have been several days. Eventually I realized I was not dreaming and reality for me had changed.

Later that day I was shown statements in large print. I responded to:

raise your thumb,
make a fist,
lift your knee,
wiggle your toes.

Fred correctly concluded that I could still read.

18 February

Statements, including the original four, were written onto cards and I quickly read and responded to them all.

20 February

I was becoming more alert, watching the television and turning the pages of the book when being read to. I was responding to both written and verbal commands.

22 February

I began to suck and swallow water from the toothbrush when my teeth were being cleaned. This was the first liquid I had taken by mouth for two months. I was unaware that I had taken a very significant step towards more independence. The resumption of the oral intake of food was now a vague possibility.

27 February
I was more alert and was able to read small print and to turn the pages of magazines by myself. Priorities were now changing, I had survived and I was no longer in a coma. The increased muscular tone and spasticity of my left side were now very important. Although advice on correct positioning was sought, the problems continued to develop. I was apparently a very bad patient and did not remain laying in the correct position!

3 March
I continued 'drinking' from my toothbrush and a speech therapist came to the ward to investigate and advise on my swallowing.

I was able to write my Christian name and indicate by pointing to letters on a chart, how to complete my full name.

4 March
Following the visit of the speech therapist a nurse wrote the following comments:

> Heather and I gave her an ice pop. Molly went at it hammer and tongs! The ice pop never stood a chance. No signs of choking. N.B. Molly had specifically asked for a lemon flavoured ice pop unfortunately we only had lime! Molly was very alert following her ice pop. She cleaned her teeth extremely well, coordination much better. Molly also gave us a lovely smile! Molly then tried to mouth a word when I asked her if she could try to speak. She was obviously frustrated, as whatever she wanted to say would not come.

This was the first of many ice pops and iced lollipops that I ate; I was unable to speak but I was able to make effective use of hand signals and pointing.

INJURY, REHABILITATION AND INSURANCE

6 March
I typed two words using a BBC computer but I was too tired to continue.

8 March
I was visited by two colleagues. Apparently, I interrogated them for one and a half hours concerning any developments at the school. I used a printed alphabet and sign language for communication, which prompted my colleague to design and construct a communication aid for me.

10 March, 01.35 a.m.
I was cold and two nurses give me an extra blanket. Using the point chart we had a long conversation and when they asked me if I wanted them to go, I said NO, then I began to utter words. These mumblings included FRED, GOOD, KATE, and WHY, with reference to the gastrostomy tube. I also showed an interest in the diary and tried to take it. The nurse wrote:

> This is definitely a night to remember!

The following evening I pointed to the clock to show I could tell the time and that I knew Fred was late.

I was visited by my headmaster. I indicated I was concerned about my job. It never occurred to me that my teaching days were over. I wonder what he thought?

11 March
The colleague delivered the communication aid, which I began to use immediately. Although using scrabble letters was very slow, I had acquired a limited method of communication.

12 March
My diet now included puréed soup and ice cream.

I was able to complete mathematical problems, play card 'Patience', noughts and crosses and Hangman.

13 March
I was agitated for most of the afternoon and evening as I knew I was to be moved to the rehabilitation unit of another hospital.

My stay in the third hospital was at an end. I had been cared for by a wonderful team of nurses, who had supported me and my family through a very difficult time. I used the communication aid to spell WORRY and had a very restless night. Fred had already spoken to the consultant, who explained to him the nature of a rehabilitation unit.

Unlike the previous moves, I was fully aware of my situation and my complete dependence on other people, so I was very frightened.

CHAPTER V

The Rehabilitation Unit

14 March

I had my first experience of the difficulties facing the ambulance service. The ward received an early message: I would be collected from the ward at nine o'clock and taken to the rehabilitation unit at the other hospital. I was actually collected at two o'clock in the afternoon and I spent the morning feeling agitated and apprehensive. A nurse accompanied me to the unit; she was concerned for my welfare and she appreciated the difficulties I faced and the fear I felt.

I was placed on the main women's ward. I can remember laying on the bed feeling desperately unhappy and very much alone, vulnerable and physically helpless. I could not move voluntarily, not even to change my position in bed. Although I could utter the odd word I could not talk effectively. I knew nobody – shortly after I arrived my nurse companion had reluctantly returned to the other hospital. I was fully aware of my situation and I felt trapped and frightened.

I could not tolerate life like this. I had been used to watching the television, even though many of the programmes I could not understand – I had cognitive problems, I suffered from double vision, was deaf in one ear and suffered tinnitus. However, when the television was on, it stopped unwelcome or destructive thoughts. I needed privacy. I had problems of my own but selfishly could not cope with the problems, or tolerate the strange behaviour of the other patients.

THE REHABILITATION UNIT

I had seen Fred in the morning but he was not allowed to travel in the ambulance. When he came to visit me in the evening I had decided on a plan of campaign. I used the communication aid, in an attempt to convey my plan to Fred. I used the letters to spell PRIVATE and BUPA (I had private health insurance).

15 March

I was in pain and uncomfortable for most of the day. With the help of a dietitian, a puréed menu was arranged for me.

Jay spent the afternoon with me. I had started to think about the cause of the accident but I knew very little. I was aware I had been a passenger in a car, and was very concerned that the driver was a member of my immediate family. I had no recollection of the St Ives visit. I, very unfairly, indicated to Jay I wanted her to tell me, which she reluctantly did. When Fred came in the evening I used the aid and we talked about the accident – not in any great detail. It was to be several years before I learned the full facts.

16 March

I received my nutritional requirements via the gastrostomy tube but I was keen, or to be more honest, impatient, to have the tube removed. I had seen the dietitian the previous day but nobody had completed a request for meals. The only item available was a pot of yoghurt. The meals system was explained to me. This was the first of many dietary problems. The most serious was finding several very large bones in puréed fish! Not once, but surprisingly twice!

I spent the next weeks getting used to life in the rehabilitation unit. The consultant told Fred I would be moved to a single room when one became available. I was unable to go to the day room, therefore we arranged to hire a television.

A weekly timetable, for each patient, was displayed on the ward. The physiotherapist asked Fred to bring tracksuits for me as I was

INJURY, REHABILITATION AND INSURANCE

to dress for each day's activities. This was the first time I had worn something other than a nightdress or a hospital gown for three months. My timetable included a daily physiotherapy session. I was unable to sit by myself therefore initially two therapists were required. I had occupational and speech therapy several times during the week.

A video was made to record my progress. Amazingly, it was the only item left by thieves when several months later they helped themselves to the contents of the hospital safe! The video could not portray my desperation, fear and anxiety.

By the end of March I could stand, if supported, for one second. I was able to bend my left leg a little, my left arm was looser and I was more communicative. For no obvious reason, each morning the right side of my face, and every evening both my knees became bright red. Visitors began to comment on a definite improvement.

Despite this improvement when Fred pushed me outside for the first time I found the experience difficult to cope with. I had accepted, or at least come to terms with, my situation when indoors – illogically this acceptance did not apply out of doors.

To be more honest, my so-called acceptance would be better called escapism. The situation I found myself in was foreign to me in every way. I hated being dependent on other people for all aspects of everyday life – I mean all aspects! The only way I was able to survive was to act.

Teaching, I think, demands giving a performance. I had always believed the children deserved a good lesson, irrespective of how I was feeling. This often required putting aside personal problems and stepping into a role. Over the years I had become a very good actress. I adopted similar techniques in my present situation. I could not deal with the real situation, so whenever possible I escaped into a situation I could manage. This situation was often to be found between the pages of a book or watching the television

THE REHABILITATION UNIT

or in my refusal to face reality. During the physiotherapy sessions, I refused to use a full-length mirror. My reflected image had no part to play in my pretence, the reflection was reality.

I was only able to survive the occupational therapy sessions if I adopted a role. I could find no reason for making scones, playing 'Beetle' or attending the patients' group. I was able to survive the many indignities of a normal day on the unit using this strategy.

I was totally unprepared for the mixture of emotions I felt when I was outside for the first time. It was the first time my pretence was seriously challenged, or was found to be wanting. I escaped back to the unit and the familiar with which I had come to terms.

A month later I was settled in my own room and a visitor wrote the following comment:

> Popped in to say hello! What a surprise, Molly looked a different lady and her progress is remarkable!

I was seen again by the dietitian, this time she decided I no longer needed to be fed by the gastrostomy tube but I still needed extra fluid and my medication delivered via the tube. Progress indeed!

I had the first of several tests by a clinical psychologist. The tests confirmed the cognitive, psychological and emotional changes I had suffered. Confirmation was easy – unfortunately confirmation did not offer a solution and the knowledge brought no relief.

I had a swallowing defect and a weak cough, my food was puréed and drinks were thickened but even so there remained a risk I might choke. I had to be supervised when eating. One more indignity!

Over time I received various gifts from the pupils at school. These included two large, framed, handmade posters and a chest filled with a hundred handmade, three-dimensional stars, with the simple message:

100 WISH YOU WELL STARS

INJURY, REHABILITATION AND INSURANCE

The gifts included several fluffy toys. One of the posters, a picture of the evening sky, included a poem:

> LIFE IS LIKE THE MOON
> IT CHANGES CONSTANTLY
> BUT ONE DAY
> IT WILL BE ITS OLD SELF AGAIN
> LIKE YOU WILL BE
> MRS DAVISON

Every member of my seventh-year science group sent me a decorated letter.

A further visit from my headmaster brought confirmation that he had made arrangements to keep my job open for a year. I now thought I knew what he had decided on his first visit, or did I?

I was also visited by colleagues. One, with whom I had organized a combined A level Geography/Biology field course in France, talked about going again.

The nurses said there must be a reason for my survival. In spite of the obvious difficulties all these things strengthened my resolve to conquer the present adversity.

My progress continued, I could now sit for ten minutes unsupported. The physiotherapist wrote:

> Molly has had excellent physiotherapy sessions for the last two days. She has stood, with the minimum amount of support, and has tried some stepping with the right leg. Molly has agreed to wear her hand splint tonight. Do you think you could put it on Fred?

This was the first of numerous hand and leg splints I wore over the following years. My left wrist was very arched causing the palm of my hand to be pulled against my forearm. When I was in a coma it had been attached to the forearm in this position. My fingers curved away from the palm so that I was unable to form a fist or use my hand, and therefore I was unable to propel a manual wheelchair.

THE REHABILITATION UNIT

At the end of May I was supplied with a small battery-powered wheelchair that could be controlled by the right hand. It was no longer necessary for the therapists to collect me for the various treatments. I should have been delighted but I was not. I still believed that if I worked hard my handicaps were only temporary. The power chair had a permanency I had not accepted, so I was not disappointed when the control mechanism proved to be faulty and it had to be returned to the manufacturer.

Three weeks later the physiotherapist wrote:

> We have decided to try hydrotherapy with Molly next week. Could she have a costume please? Molly took her first few steps today with some support from me and lightly holding on to the table. Did extremely well.

My left Achilles tendon was very tight so that it was impossible for me to put my foot flat on the ground. Despite this difficulty I started to use the parallel bars, and by the beginning of July I had walked the length of the bars, turned round and walked back.

I was having regular sessions of speech therapy but I was still very difficult to understand. These sessions included advice on the oral intake of liquids and food. To allow further investigation of my swallowing mechanism, the speech therapist made arrangements for videofluoroscopy of the throat. This technique confirmed that food and liquids tended to pool at the back of my throat and some droplets went down the trachea, which inevitably caused coughing. Once again confirmation was easy but, as before, it did not provide a solution.

At the end of July plans for my eventual discharge began. The unit was accustomed to the rehabilitation of long-stay patients – there was a tried and tested path. Little was asked of me and I asked little. I was happy to go along with whatever was decided. I had no idea of the problems I had before me. Neither I nor anyone else, as time was about to show, had a realistic knowledge of my injuries or the future I could expect, or if they had, they did not tell me.

My physiotherapist considered that with regular physiotherapy, I would eventually walk short distances; my headmaster was keeping my job open. I did not pursue the problems, it was very much a case of: where ignorance is bliss 'tis folly to be wise. I was surprised plans were starting for my discharge as I was a long way from being recovered, so I did not pursue this line of thought.

The discharge plans commenced with a short home visit. I experienced the same mixture of emotions I had suffered when going outside for the first time, and could not handle my handicapped condition in surroundings I associated with normality. I returned to the haven of the unit very depressed. The nursing staff tried to help and presented me with a framed certificate.

Certificate of 'still gots'
awarded to Molly Davison
who has still got
her youthful good looks *
her lovely red hair *
determination, dignity and self respect *
a great sense of humour *
the knack of finding bones in hospital puréed fish *
lots and lots of people who care and love her dearly especially Fred a husband in a million *
a lot of hard work ahead but with these STILL GOTS will succeed.
Presented by the nursing staff of the rehabilitation unit
1st August 1994.

August brought more changes. The gastrostomy tube was removed and the plans for my eventual discharge entered the next phase when I went home for a full day. The only way I could travel

THE REHABILITATION UNIT

the short distance to my home was sitting in my wheelchair in the back of a black cab with my eyes firmly closed. The day visits were repeated and one was used by the physiotherapist and the occupational therapist to ascertain what had to be purchased and what arrangements had to be made before my eventual discharge.

At the end of August I detected for the first time when the toes of my left foot touched the ground, although I was still not able to detect contact with the rest of my foot. I had managed, with the help of the physiotherapist and the hand rail, to climb three steps.

Thankfully, September brought more changes: I was able to walk a short distance with the combined support of the physiotherapist and a walking stick, and was able to stand for a few seconds with only the support of the walking stick.

My planned discharge continued when I stayed overnight at home, but I was unable to go upstairs so I slept in the dining room. Fred brought a single bed downstairs and combined with the pressure-relief mattresses we brought with us from the unit, we managed. I had a whistle to wake Fred if I needed him during the night. He slept nearby on a mattress on the floor. I did not allow myself to address the true situation – I was at home again for one night, at the time that was all that mattered.

I continued to use big black cabs to travel home and made the journey several times before I dared to open my eyes. I was catapulted into making the next step when the driver of a black cab, booked to return me to the hospital, refused to take me in the wheelchair. I can only assume that he did not want to put up the ramps to allow me to board. I saw the tail lights of the taxi disappear – I was supposed to be back on the unit before the outer door was locked. The only way to get there was to use our own car. Fortunately Kathryn was at home, so we telephoned the unit to warn them of the delay. With Kathryn's help I managed to get into the back seat of the car and the hospital staff met the car to help me get out.

INJURY, REHABILITATION AND INSURANCE

Following a course of relaxation, I am now able to control the fear. If I open my eyes, I suffer from double vision and can see oncoming traffic in the field as well as on the road, and an additional line in the middle of the road diverging from the central line. The vibration of the car adversely affects my tinnitus. These effects, combined with pain and hemiplegia make riding as a passenger unpleasant and driving myself impossible.

By the end of October I was able to walk a short distance with only the support of the physiotherapist and no walking stick. Throughout November Fred implemented the advice of the occupational therapists and the house, far from ideal for a disabled person, was made ready for my eventual discharge: a stair lift was fitted.

I was discharged on 25 November, having been in hospital for almost a year.

The legal process, started when I was a patient in Addenbrookes Hospital, had to reflect my changing medical condition and also respond to the actions of the insurance company and their solicitors – the 'other side'!

Their first response to a claim for damages was the accusation that I had not been wearing a properly fitted or adjusted seat belt and that I had contributed to my injuries through my own negligence. This was done in the form of a formal response made to the court when my case was first set down on 9 January 1995.

> It would be alleged by the Defendant that to such extent as the injuries, loss and damage may be proved by the Plaintiff such injuries, loss and damage were caused or contributed to by the negligence of the Plaintiff in that she failed to wear a properly fitted or adjusted seat belt whilst travelling in the said motor vehicle and thereby failed to take any or any other good precaution for her safety.

I had no recollection of the accident and was very upset by the accusation because I had always worn a seat belt and insisted that

THE REHABILITATION UNIT

other members of my family always did. My son declared, 'You are bound to have been wearing a belt. You make me wear one when the car is stationary in the drive!'

My injuries were consistent with wearing a belt. The solicitor pointed out the police report and the ambulance men had indicated I was wearing a seat belt. I find it hard to believe the insurance company would fail to read the police report. However, I do know any compensation would be substantially reduced if I had not taken basic steps to reduce serious injury.

There were further comments, which would assume monumental importance in the following years:

> For the purposes of this action and not otherwise the Defendant admits his liability to pay damages for injuries, loss and damage as the Plaintiff may prove to have resulted from the collision complained of in the Particulars of Claim.
>
> The extent of the alleged injuries, loss and damage claimed is not admitted and the Plaintiff is put to proof thereof.

The following account details my medical state on discharge. Although the report that forms the basis for these observations was prepared at the end of September I had changed little.

My cognitive skills and memory were impaired and I was unable to have a normal conversation. All my food had to be puréed and liquids thickened. I was depressed and very anxious. I had a clear insight into my losses and I felt very bleak about the future.

I suffered persistent severe left spastic hemiplegia and dysphagia that affected facial movements and movements throughout the left side. I had double vision and a small divergent squint. My left eye did not respond to light. Movement of my tongue and palate remained slow.

I was unable to use my left side functionally and I was unable to coordinate any movements of my left hand. I was unable to move from my chair to the bed without assistance. I could not move in bed and I therefore required assistance to change position. I needed assistance with meals, dressing and bathing.

I had not regained a normal sleep rhythm. I required twice-weekly phosphate enemas.

CHAPTER VI

December 1994-December 1995

Settling down to a changed lifestyle was very difficult. My weekly activities now included spending two days at a Resource Centre, which provided opportunities for a variety of activities. Personally, these included cooking, sewing, computing and a speech group.

I attended the hospital's physiotherapy department on the three additional weekdays. The hospital was only half a mile away from the house but the entire excursion could take up to five hours for the hour therapy session. I became a regular addition to the hospital coffee bar, waiting for the ambulance to take me home. The excursion often included lengthy trips around the housing estates of Reading, dropping off or picking up patients for both Reading hospitals.

I spent the remainder of the weekdays with agency carers so I looked forward to the weekends. I did not allow myself to compare my present life with what had gone before. If my mind wandered I made a hasty readjustment.

In the hospital I had benefited from daily physiotherapy but the new routine did not provide for this and I soon lost mobility. To help alleviate the situation my physiotherapist came to the Resource Centre and showed the staff how to walk with me. This helped, but did not solve the problem.

I was very confused. I began to think my expectation of improvement was unrealistic. Certainly, the move home had had a disastrous effect on this objective. If life now was to consist of two days at the Resource Centre and three days with agency carers, which included the lengthy trips to hospital, I wanted no part of it. However, I was too incapacitated to do anything about it, as I could not talk about it, and at this stage I could not use the computer for communication, therefore the situation continued. My frustration increased and I was totally helpless, an able mind frustrated by a disabled body, trapped in an impossible situation.

Shortly after discharge, I made arrangements to return to the school to see my tutor group. I had always given each member a card and a very small gift for Christmas. I intended to resume the tradition and thank them for their support, not thinking about or beyond the event. The headmaster was aware of my intention and Fred went with me.

The school buildings are old and they are not wheelchair friendly. The staff room was on the second floor and steps were a feature of most of the corridors. Fred was given help to lift me, sitting in the wheelchair, up the three steps at the entrance. The headmaster had asked my tutor group to assemble in the small hall near the main entrance.

I should have thought about the logistics and the emotional impact of my intention. To write 'things were difficult' does not begin to describe my feelings or the reactions of the pupils. My tutor group was of mixed ability and reflected the multi-ethnic nature of the area. Many of the pupils had asked to see me when I was in hospital but had been discouraged. A few had breached my defences, but for most of them, apart from the early progress reports, this was the first time they had had to face the consequences of a serious road accident.

The meeting had no structure and no agenda. All the participants, including me, had no prior experience to provide clues to expected behaviour. Many of the pupils found my handicapped condition and multiple injuries difficult to handle. With hindsight, I realized, they must have been involved in a mental comparison of the before and after person. I left with various scenes indelibly printed on my brain: the seated circle of unusually quiet pupils, my inadequacy, the maturity of the pupil who took charge of the proceedings, the long line of pupils collecting the small gift as they left the hall, the mumbled responses of a few of them.

Life goes on – or so they say – and in an attempt to resume a more normal life, Jay and Matthew bought tickets for a performance at the Hexagon Theatre in Reading. They accompanied Fred and I. It was the first time, since the accident, I had been into a crowded place with a lot of background noise. My ears buzzed loudly, my head throbbed and my vision was disturbed. I could not filter out, or ignore, the background noise during the intervals or when in the public rooms. Double vision, tinnitus, anxiety and pain all conspired to make the evening very difficult. I was relieved when the performance ended. My discomfort didn't. I saw the rehabilitation consultant and she suggested seeing a number of experts. Once again they were able to confirm my many problems, but to alleviate them was completely different, and a much more difficult task.

At the beginning of June my physiotherapist resigned from her post. I was devastated. She had worked with me when I was in the rehabilitation unit and for six months as an outpatient. In addition to a great personal loss her departure caused a shortage of trained physiotherapists at the hospital.

Fred had acted on the advice of the occupational therapist and he had made the house ready for my discharge, but many insurmountable problems remained:
- The house was approached by a steep drive.
- In the kitchen the work surfaces were at standard height, with cupboards or drawers beneath; there was no room for a wheelchair. Many of the appliances I could not use. I could not reach the wall cupboards.

- The stairlift tracking at the curved section of the flight of steps rendered the stairs unsafe for normal use.
- There was a series of steps into the back garden, which I could view from the conservatory but I could not enter by this route.
- The only door I could use was the front door, which was blocked by the heavy hinged section of tracking when the stairlift was in use.
- Access to the downstairs cloakroom and the study were restricted.
- I could not enter two of the bedrooms, the en suite bathroom or the utility room.

My world, when at home, had become the bedroom, family bathroom, lounge, dining room and the conservatory.

Moving house became a priority and deflected my attention from the physiotherapy situation. I welcomed the distraction now I could enjoy normal activities, activities I had pursued when able bodied. This allowed a pattern of behaviour to develop which would persist for several years. I gave my attention to the changes I could make to my physical environment. This strategy allowed me to ignore my disability or, at the very least, what I did acknowledge I believed I could minimize with yet one more change.

I was involved in a court case, in which the defendant had admitted liability, which allowed Fred and I to negotiate a huge bank loan. After searching for several months we found a property. I employed a firm of architects, with experience in building for disabled people, to assess the bungalow's suitability and then to plan and oversee any necessary alterations.

My life seemed to revolve around several areas: therapies; the impending move; the bungalow conversions; my care; health problems; and the legal matters. Each area demanded my attention and I found it impossible to meet all the diverse demands; many I ignored. I responded to the most pressing which, with the benefit

DECEMBER 1994-DECEMBER 1995

The bungalow.

of hindsight, I can now see were not the most important. At the time, my response allowed me to continue with my pretence, and I was not required to address the real situation.

Fred and I already had a mortgage on our existing house, we were facing large building costs and now we had a huge bank loan. From our behaviour, the casual observer would think we were involved in a game of monopoly, literally owing over a hundred and twenty thousand pounds here, another hundred thousand pounds there and only the odd seventy thousand pounds elsewhere. The bungalow was fifteen miles from Reading but nearer to Fred's workplace. We knew we would have to be available at the site from time to time. After consideration of all these facts, we decided to try to sell our house and move to the bungalow. Life in a building site would be preferable to the financial worry of owning two properties... or so I thought. At the very least Fred would have an easier drive to work and we would both be available on the site at all times. I needed the distraction.

Unfortunately, we were trying to sell the house in a depressed market, having purchased the bungalow in more favourable times. We also realized that until the conversion was complete we could

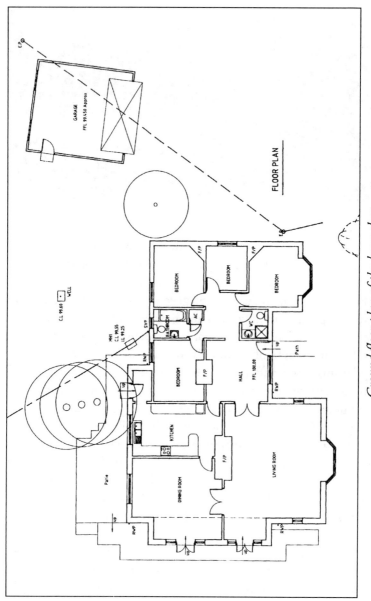

Ground floor plan of the bungalow.

DECEMBER 1994-DECEMBER 1995

not employ a live-in carer. We would have to use agency carers for the hours I was at home and Fred was at work. Fred agreed to continue to provide the additional care.

In an attempt to straighten the very arched shape of the middle finger of my left hand I was wearing a finger splint. The splint did not appear to be making any difference to the shape of my finger but it did restrict the blood circulation. The physiotherapist suggested attempting to correct the permanently arched wrist first. I was surprised there was not a tried and tested procedure. Surely, I could not be the first person with this problem? Could they not seek help? Why was the occupational therapist making the splint? It was an occasion when I should have complained, but I didn't.

The physiotherapist assigned to me was attending a lengthy course and the department was already short of therapists so my appointments were cut to two per week. My mobility reduced, and I was unable to take one step, with or without the help of the therapist and a supporting tripod. The spasticity and the pain increased. Over the Christmas period the physiotherapy sessions suffered further reductions.

Every area of my life seemed beset with problems and I became very depressed. I felt like a juggler who had too many balls to juggle. My counsellor's advise was not to be influenced by events I could do nothing about, but to become involved with something I could influence. This advice has been my salvation on numerous occasions – on this occasion, it resulted in this book and a letter to my consultant to make her aware of the physiotherapy situation.

The rest of this book details in chronological order my attempt to juggle the 'balls'. On waking each morning there they all were. If I did not pick them up, I had given up. The consequences of such an action would allow the prognosis formulated in Cambridge to become fact. If I picked them up, who knows?

CHAPTER VII

January-February 1996

The new year brought some welcome changes. In response to my letter, the consultant arranged for my readmittance into the rehabilitation unit for three weeks of intensive physiotherapy.

The physiotherapy department was still short of staff, therefore intensive physiotherapy became what the department was physically able to provide. This amounted to a one-hour therapy session each day, supplemented on some days by standing in the standing frame or stretching exercises on the bed.

As before I worked with the occupational therapists. On different days I baked, played 'beetle' or used the computer, but for most of the day I read or watched the television.

I went home each evening, returning before eight o'clock the following morning. At the end of the first week I had walked one step by myself. The physiotherapists did not work at weekends therefore I returned home.

The following Monday my therapist was ill so I had no physiotherapy.

I did see the speech therapist and she suggested compiling all the recipes I used into a booklet. This could be used by fellow sufferers of dysphagia. I was pleased to do this as it concurred with the notion of doing something I could influence. I made an immediate start.

My physiotherapist returned to work. At the end of the three-week period I was again able to walk a short distance with the minimum of support, using a tripod as a walking aid. There was an improvement in my posture, attributed to the increased use of the standing frame. Arrangements commenced to have one made for home use.

Regular physiotherapy had certainly improved my mobility and it had reduced the pain and spasticity. The consultant recommended daily physiotherapy. Unfortunately, reality was very different from the recommendation. The department remained short of staff and my therapist was attending a course lasting the whole of the following week, so the sessions were cancelled. I should have sought a solution to the lack of physiotherapy and did not appreciate the seriousness of my situation.

The house sale was proving difficult. We were at the end of a long chain which suffered the usual breakage. We began to use more estate agents and towards the end of January we thought the chain was complete so we began to plan the move. The alterations required to make the bungalow suitable for a person with my disabilities went to five local builders for tenders.

Our house in Reading had a fully-fitted kitchen with a full range of built-in appliances, features not enjoyed by the bungalow. Our chest freezer, in the garage, was over twenty-five years old and the removal firm warned us it was unlikely to survive another move. Our house had four very full, fitted wardrobes, the bungalow had none. A shopping spree was essential! We bought a small refrigerator, a combination microwave oven, an upright freezer and a long clothes rail.

The fitted carpets and curtains we had purchased with the bungalow bore the evidence of heavy smoking and a large dog. My husband staggered to the dry cleaners with the curtains, and the family descended upon the bungalow armed with the necessary equipment and cleaning materials for all the carpets, windows, doors, bathrooms and the kitchen.

I worked on scale plans to try to accommodate all our furniture into the lounge, dining room and one of the small bedrooms. This arrangement would allow the builders to start work on the conversion. Fred split the water plants and bought large plastic pots to accommodate half of them, then took the plastic pots and some of the pot plants to the bungalow.

The new year brought changes to the legal situation: my case was being handled by a different solicitor as my first solicitor had left the practice. I think at this stage, it is necessary to share with you my understanding of litigation.

My solicitor requested a number of medical experts to comment on the changes the accident had brought to my life, to assess the future implications of these changes and to write a report. I saw a wide range of medical experts, ten in all. I also obtained reports from an occupational therapist and an architect. Both these experts considered the financial implications of the provisions recommended by the medical experts. All of these reports were disclosed to the 'other side' and then forwarded to a forensic accountant to produce a schedule of financial loss.

The schedule of financial loss is divided into two sections. The first section was concerned with those financial losses and expenses incurred before the settlement. The second section predicted future financial losses and expenses that would be incurred after the settlement.

The 'other side' could either accept the disclosed experts' reports or request their own reports, written by experts of their own choosing. When the schedule of loss was presented, the 'other side' had two additional weeks to produce a counter schedule of loss, using our disclosed reports and any reports they had commissioned. Any new reports had to be disclosed to us.

If there was agreement between the two schedules, an amount would be added for pain and suffering and an additional amount to cover the interest lost on the total settlement since the case was first set down. If there was no agreement between the two schedules and an agreement could not be reached out of court, the case would go to court and the settlement would be decided by a judge.

I understood the function of the reports was to assess reality: I had to endeavour to mitigate the losses of the insurance company and not to seek betterment of my financial circumstances. It was important to accurately assess reality: my injuries are extensive, and necessitated the full range of experts' reports. This was my understanding of litigation, but I am no lawyer!

The report by our occupational therapist was considered by the defendant's insurance company to be too costly. They requested a further report by their own expert. My life expectancy was an issue for them as this could make a huge difference to the size of the award. Put bluntly, I would need less money for my care if my early death was expected! A letter in June 1995 had stated:

> Obviously, the question of life expectancy will be a key feature of this claim and this will no doubt be covered in due course.

This preoccupation with my life expectancy had a profound effect on me. I had often heard the expression 'life is short'; of course I knew its meaning, but up until now I had not really appreciated its significance. Now, I most certainly did. People were actively involved calculating my 'sell-by date'.

I had not considered life after Fred's death. I know life expectancy for a woman is longer than for a man, but again I did not consider its implications.

I was now required to consider both concepts and their financial implications. The result – never again would I be able to enjoy the day and look ahead to the future. Life was now very finite and each day needed to be provided for. Herein lay the problems. What constituted my life? How much care did I need and for how many years? Which therapies did I need and for how long? I was advised by my solicitor to seek the help of a senior QC.

Also included in their June 1995 letter was the following statement:

> We also seek your permission to instruct an architect to examine your client's present property.

At the end of January of the following year the Defendant's insurance company made a request to inspect 'the property'. We agreed, although they did not make it clear which property they wished to inspect!

My solicitor informed the Defendant's solicitors of our impending move. As had happened on previous occasions, and was to be a regular feature of the case, she received no immediate reply. We made arrangements to take a video of the house to illustrate those problems which made a move essential. The 'other side' did not inspect the house nor did they inspect the bungalow.

From a consultant, an orthopaedic and trauma specialist, I learned in detail about the damage to my pelvis and the shortened left leg. The other injuries I was already only too aware of.

CHAPTER VIII

March-April 1996

March had a very positive beginning and I was reaping the benefit of three weekly sessions of physiotherapy. The staffing situation, despite the consultant's recommendation, would not allow therapy any more often. I was now able to walk around a series of cones using my tripod but without any support from the physiotherapist.

This positive phase was soon replaced by another session of conflicting demands. I responded in the usual way and the most pressing, but not necessarily the most important, received my attention, any that could be left I ignored.

My physiotherapist went on a holiday, sessions were reduced again and I could only be seen by a helper. I began to suffer additional pain in my left leg and foot. The helper was unsure what was causing the added pain – she had neither medical nor physiotherapy qualifications. I should have made a fuss, but I didn't. I had other demands on my time and other problems to deal with. These other problems were those experienced by able-bodied people; I preferred finding a solution to these problems, the others I foolishly ignored.

Our purchaser's buyers were storing their furniture in a friend's office who now required the office. We were asked to store the furniture, but our solicitor advised refusal. When this issue was resolved we faced a further complication when our purchaser required a medical before he could obtain a mortgage.

INJURY, REHABILITATION AND INSURANCE

We had already made arrangements for the move so we decided to go ahead, although the contracts had not been exchanged. Having made this irrevocable decision it began snowing. My sister, who had agreed to help with the move, was attending a business conference in York. The weather was so bad, the conference ended early and all the normal restrictions on rail travel were lifted, so she arrived in Reading earlier than we had expected to see her.

The snow came quickly and disappeared just as quickly. Before the move could commence the stairlift was removed, confining me to the ground floor. On both days of the move I went to physiotherapy, leaving Fred to organize the packing of the boxes and the emptying of the house. My sister went to the bungalow taking my scale drawings with her; the removal van shuttled between the two properties. After the physiotherapy session on the second day Fred and I went to the bungalow.

The removal company had estimated two days for the complete removal. Towards the end of the second day it became obvious that the move was much bigger than the company had thought. When the removal van finally left the bungalow we were surrounded by 141 boxes and all our furniture! In the garage there was a heap of hastily removed, roughly folded carpets. The removal men had failed to move the contents of the utility room and many of the light fittings remained in the house. It was fortunate the contracts had not been exchanged!

The next few days were very difficult. Somehow we managed to find our way to the beds. Fred and I slept in the dining room surrounded by furniture and boxes. My sister slept in one of the small bedrooms, also surrounded by furniture.

My plans had not considered the effect of 141 boxes, the three wheelchairs and the various disability aids! In the lounge there was a wall of over a hundred very large boxes. The wall, several boxes deep, stretched across the entire room and was at least six feet high, completely obliterating the sight of the very large fireplace. The room also contained a collection of a large proportion of our furniture, with not a square foot of floor space.

Of the remaining three small rooms, one acted as a store for disability aids and a wheelchair park; the other two, as I had planned, were empty – I did get something right!

The chaos I saw before me was the only logical outcome of an attempt to accommodate the contents of a house with four bedrooms, three reception rooms and a conservatory, into three rooms and a hall.

We tackled the boxes first. I say we, what I actually mean is my husband and sister did all the manual work, my role was planning. One by one the 141 boxes were unpacked, their contents sorted and then repacked with the things we could manage without during the conversion. The boxes were temporarily stacked in one of the empty bedrooms. Matthew, Jay and Kathryn came to help roll the carpets that had been so unceremoniously removed from the house which allowed them to be properly wrapped and stored in the garage.

When we finally took my sister to Reading station for her return journey, we collected the remaining items from the house and received the welcome news that the contracts had been exchanged.

At a site meeting with the builders and the architect, we were told the builders planned to begin work towards the end of April. They proposed dividing the house with a screen. On one side, our side, we would have access to the lounge, dining room, hall, kitchen, one small bedroom, a bathroom and a shower room. On the other side, the builder's side, they would have access to the other three bedrooms and the land for the new bedroom-bathroom complex. When the builders had completed work on their side, we would exchange sides. This would allow completion of the carer's accommodation, refitting of the main kitchen and the family bathroom and the widening of all the doorways. This

INJURY, REHABILITATION AND INSURANCE

was the theoretical plan, time would tell whether it would work in practice!

This was not the only theoretical plan. Prior to the move, I thought I had arranged how I could continue to attend the Resource Centre on two days and the physiotherapy department for the three sessions. I planned to use the Readibus, a service for elderly and disabled people, to go to the Resource Centre and the ambulance service for the return journey. For the third physiotherapy session I intended to use the ambulance service. Cold Ash is in the area served by the Reading hospitals and the ambulance service was informed of the move. To reduce the number of times I would have to travel between Cold Ash and Reading, the staff at the Resource Centre agreed to transport me to physiotherapy when their day was complete.

There were difficulties with the theoretical plan. The ambulance service could not bring me home if the physiotherapy session finished later than 2.00 p.m. There were certain days I could not have a late physiotherapy appointment.

I planned to solve these problems by using a taxi. I had been advised to mitigate the losses of the insurance company. The cost of the taxi was significantly less than the cost of care for the two days. I intended to travel alone, using the taxi to take me home from the hospital after the late physiotherapy session. I also used a taxi to take me from the Resource Centre on the previous day when late physiotherapy was impossible. I planned to go to and from physiotherapy on two days using the ambulance service.

I thought I had covered all eventualities, however on the first day I was due to be collected by the ambulance, it failed to arrive. I made enquiries and learned the ambulance service had no record of my existence. I had to be treated as a new patient and it would take several days to sort out – what can you say?

The pattern of the physiotherapy sessions was eventually established as I had planned. At the beginning of April I was able

MARCH-APRIL 1996

to walk 10 metres in 6 minutes and 46 seconds, with only my tripod as an aid. The following week the walking did not go well, but I managed to climb up and down a flight of stairs. Not in the conventional way, as I could not get out of the wheelchair without a great deal of help, so I made use of the banister and the physiotherapist stood beside me on every step, but I did get up and down the stairs.

The fifteen-mile journey to attend the physiotherapy session was proving to be a very lengthy excursion. The ambulance station was in Newbury, therefore I was usually the first patient to be collected. On the way into Reading the ambulance collected patients for the outpatients' clinics of both Reading hospitals. On the return journey, as well as returning patients to their homes, the ambulance crew collected patients for the Newbury hospital. Personally, this usually meant I was collected from my home at 8.30 a.m. and returned at about 2.00 p.m. I had learned to manage a similar frustrating situation when living in Reading. However, when the ambulance was late arriving at the hospital, my one-hour session was shortened, as my physiotherapist had to treat other patients. I was grateful I could still read. An additional effect of the brain injury is that I never feel either hunger or thirst, and my medication can be delayed by several hours – other patients were less fortunate.

To increase the amount of physiotherapy I was receiving, I paid to attend a local hydrotherapy pool. I went weekly and travelled by taxi. A carer went with me to help with dressing and to provide support in the pool in order to assist the physiotherapist.

I was depressed, tired and had little stamina, the whole of my left side was painful and my left foot swollen. In an attempt to eliminate the effects of double vision, I was prescribed glasses with one frosted 'lens', which allowed me to dispense with the black eye patch. My son helped me refamiliarize myself with the computer which I used to write this book and the recipe booklet.

April ended, as it had begun, with physiotherapy suffering cancellations. The promised locum physiotherapist had not yet started work. In-patients had priority to the time of the available therapists hence a further reduction in the number of sessions.

CHAPTER IX

May-June 1996

At the end of April the builders moved in. A telephone line was diverted to the workmen's hut, the dividing screen was erected, all the boxes were stored in the garage and ramps were fitted over a section of the drive – pushing a wheelchair over gravel is an impossible task!

The original bungalow was built in 1932 on the edge of a large estate, providing accommodation for the estate's gardener. Over the following years times changed, the estate was divided into several plots and sold for development. This move separated the house from the gardener's cottage.

The cottage was compact, water was pumped from a well in the garden and it was heated by several coal fires. The drains ran into a septic tank. The previous owner had extended the property, installed oil-fired central heating and the property now enjoyed a mains water supply but had retained the septic tank.

We proposed to further extend the property, building a bedroom-bathroom complex suitable for a person with my level of disability; adapt the present accommodation to provide a self-contained carer's flat; replace the oil boiler with a larger capacity gas boiler; make all the approaches to the bungalow 'wheelchair friendly'; construct raised beds to allow me to continue gardening and replace all the windows and doors with double-glazed units as I am sedentary and soon feel the cold.

The beginning of the month heralded a brief respite from the

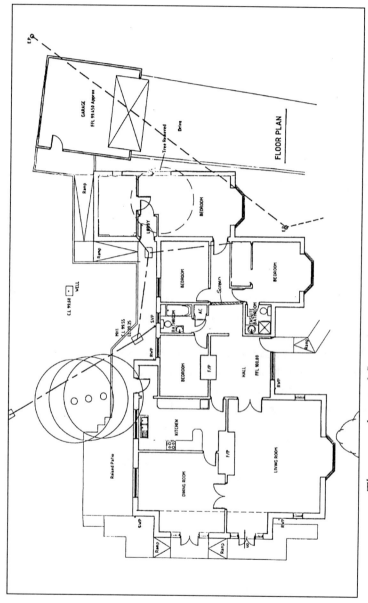

The proposed ground floor planning showing the position of the screen.

MAY-JUNE 1996

physiotherapy problems when a locum physiotherapist started working at the hospital, which allowed me to return to the thrice-weekly sessions.

However three weeks later I went as usual from the Resource Centre to discover my therapist was attending a meeting, so there was only time for a twenty-minute session when the meeting concluded. The following day therapy was reduced to another twenty-minute session with the locum physiotherapist. On the third day the ambulance was late for the appointment and as I was due to see an occupational therapist about a splint for my hand, the physiotherapy session was again reduced.

I was in pain and losing mobility. As I sat waiting for the ambulance, I mentally compared the consultant's recommendation for daily therapy with the amount I was actually receiving.

The month ended with an attempt to fix my left foot and leg in a 'better position'. The whole of the physiotherapy session was devoted to the task. After manipulation of my foot and ankle a plaster caste was made of my entire lower limb. The caste was cut to enable a back and a front splint to be made, but the following day brought disappointment as the splints were not finished.

June began and the saga of the leg splint continued. When I wore the entire splint for a relatively short time, pressure marks developed on my leg. I was asked to return the splint if this happened. The following day I spent a large part of the session laying on the bed wearing the newly padded splint. Pressure marks appeared again. The front part was thrown away and I attempted to use bandage and the back splint to hold my toe down and my leg in a better position.

Towards the middle of June I saw the consultant. She was aware that the hospital commitments were such that as an outpatient they were unable to give me the amount of physiotherapy I needed. She thought both my hand and leg splints could be improved and arrangements were made to repeat the videofluoroscopy.

Once again I followed the counsellor's advice and concentrated on those affairs I could influence – the building work occupied my mind for much of the time.

The surveyor was amazed by the construction of the original gardener's cottage although it had stood for over sixty-five years. Modern building regulations demand footings deeper than ten inches! The underpinning of the original bungalow walls was complete, the chimney breasts in two of the bedrooms were removed and the rubble was used as hardcore for the extension. A doorway was cut into the small bedroom, which would in time form a corridor to the new bedroom-bathroom complex.

As the end of the June approached the back wall of the extension was complete, the side wall was high, but not yet complete. Special bricks had arrived for the bay window and the front wall had reached floor level.

The new kitchen units were being made by a local firm, who had experience installing kitchens for the disabled. I spend a great deal of time in the kitchen. I was aware of the concept of betterment, therefore provision for this room was removed from the builder's contract. I spent many happy hours designing the layout for the new kitchen.

The extension was to be constructed on land immediately behind a telegraph pole. This pole supported a cable which brought power to our bungalow and the neighbouring house. The builders had arranged to remove the pole and lay an underground cable; the cable duly arrived on an enormous reel, which joined the confused scene. Meanwhile the drains for the new bathroom were laid across what had been the back garden.

Planning for a time which appeared to be a long way into the future, Fred and I visited a 'motability show' for the disabled. We arranged to order a Volkswagen Sharan. This car could be adapted to allow a wheelchair to board by the back door and then be secured in position. It could be driven by a carer. We also arranged

MAY-JUNE 1996

Underpinning the foundations.

to purchase a Mangar wheelchair, a chair which could rise vertically, eliminating the need for the kitchen units to be made at a special height. Both of these purchases were destined to play a very significant part in my life – not for their utility, but in the legal process!

The end of June proved to be a very significant time and heralded many changes – my physiotherapist was moving house, she therefore needed leave to see solicitors and for the move itself; sessions were cancelled.

Laying the new foundations.

The 27th of June was a very eventful day. It followed a period when everything that causes cancellation or delays to the physiotherapy sessions had occurred. I was therefore very conscious of the time. I was collected at 8.40 a.m. and after the usual collection of patients I arrived at the hospital at 10.10 a.m. My therapist was working on the wards, and when she arrived in the gymnasium she had to help another therapist with a patient.

The session began at 10.50 a.m. – I had left the bungalow two hours previously. I was now unable to take one step without support and my overall mobility was very poor, indicating the veracity of the consultant's recommendation. The hour session, which had begun late, ended early when an occupational therapist came to try to improve the hand splint. The attempt was unsuccessful.

Physiotherapy was cancelled for the whole of the following week. As I sat waiting for the ambulance I decided, 'this visit is my last visit'. I arrived home at 1.50 p.m. A superhuman effort was needed to stop myself thinking what might have been – what had been ... maybe it was a good thing I was unable to vocalize my thoughts, or was it?

On the legal front things were also happening. Fred and my solicitor travelled to London to meet with the senior QC who had agreed to represent me if the case went to trial. The journey to and across London and the geography of the Temple made it impossible for me to go. The meeting was useful, requiring immediate action in two areas.

He suggested family members, one of my husband's colleagues and both Fred and I should write witness statements. These statements should outline the changes the accident had caused. He also suggested asking for another interim settlement. I had requested the initial, interim settlement to cover the expenses incurred at the time of the accident, only asking for reimbursement of what my family had actually spent. During the trauma of the accident, the last thing on my husband's mind had been the collection of receipts or the retention of bloodstained, shredded garments, yet these items and the receipts were considered essential for the claim to be met. The response of the 'other side' was:

> For whose purpose the accommodation was provided – supply copies of receipts – reason why such expense should be borne by the defendant.
>
> Meals – providing receipts and identifying for whom the said meals were purchased and why it is considered the defendant should bear the cost thereof.
>
> Insofar as the clothing is concerned, has any of this been retained for inspection, if so let us know where it can be seen.
>
> 13.1. Rail fares – stating for whose benefit the said fares were incurred – providing receipts for the said fares – stating why it is deemed necessary for the defendant to meet the expense of such fares.

INJURY, REHABILITATION AND INSURANCE

The day of the transfer from Cambridge to Reading. Did Fred or I benefit? Was it necessary? We learned from this experience and collected receipts for absolutely everything.

I followed the QC's advice and sought another interim settlement. Again, despite the receipts, expenses were only partially met. Any expense which was considered by the insurers not to be essential was not met. The need for the purchase of items seemed to be completely arbitrary. This perspective applied to the payment of all subsequent interim settlements.

CHAPTER X

July-December 1996

My weekly routine changed dramatically, my juggling 'balls' reflecting this change. I no longer needed to address the problems associated with the lengthy journeys in the ambulance, the physiotherapy sessions or the various splints. However, other 'balls' quickly took their place.

The builders had been with us for two months, all was proceeding as they had outlined in their plan and they were making progress with the building project.

I arranged to attend a private physiotherapy clinic and to continue going to hydrotherapy. Using the facilities at the Resource Centre I carried on receiving a massage from the ICU aromatherapist, travelling alone by either taxi or the Readibus. I organized agency care around these times. My husband continued to provide the care, every evening, weekend, bank holidays and all of his annual leave. This arrangement allowed him to continue with his work, I received the therapies, the building project advanced and I required the minimum amount of care in order to mitigate the losses of the insurance company.

The plan was very complicated, my juggling required great skill and determination and Fred needed patience, stamina and understanding. When everything and everybody worked according to plan all was well, but it only required the slightest hitch and the whole elaborate construction came tumbling down and the juggling 'balls' rolled away. Total collapse was not infrequent! If as a

Progress?

reader you find the account confusing, believe me, as a participant, it was more so!

Within two weeks of receiving physiotherapy at the clinic I shuffled four steps with the minimum of support. I tried to sit down from a standing position and to roll over when laid down. The tripod and the splints were discarded, and I was provided with a professionally made splint for my hand.

Legal matters were never far away. The insurance company questioned the conclusions reached in our care report and made arrangements for their own report. I was visited by a medical services consultant. On the basis of a brief conversation, lasting no more than two hours, she assessed, for them, my requirements as she saw them.

The insurers also disputed our medical report and wished me to be seen by a doctor of their choosing, although they appeared to have some difficulty in naming a doctor. Their first suggestion was the consultant I was using. Our solicitor pointed out to them that this would be inappropriate because this consultant had written the report under dispute. Their second choice, a gastric specialist, considered he could not comment on complex neurological problems. July ended before a doctor had been named. I believed that the comments of their doctor would be important. Time would show medical comments had little bearing on the process but at this time I still held to my misguided belief. There was no mention of all the other experts' reports. These to my knowledge were not repeated by experts of their choosing. I saw nobody and no reports were disclosed.

Meanwhile the bungalow extension was continuing to take shape. A ditch was dug to accommodate the mains electricity cable. The ditch extended from the neighbour's property, through our property, down our drive, down the shared part of the drive and across the road to meet another telegraph pole – a considerable distance.

The architect was very concerned about the size of the three

And it grew and grew.

JULY-DECEMBER 1996

conifer trees several yards from the kitchen door. Fred employed a tree surgeon to assess this situation and the condition of all the conifers on the land. He waited several weeks before he commenced work. The delay was to allow a family of young magpies to leave their nest. The three mature conifers which towered above the bungalow were felled and their roots removed creating an enormous crater. The property began to look like the site of an archaeological dig! It changed further when the height of a thirty-foot row of fourteen conifers was reduced. One tree was left at its original height to allow a brood of pigeon fledglings to mature. I wondered what consternation this splendid isolation would cause to the parents and the offspring. Apparently none as the parents continued to provide food for their offspring. The fledglings eventually left the nest, the tree surgeons returned and the tree was lowered.

This work generated a mountain of logs, we used some to light our first fire and many we stored. However we were delighted when friends agreed to collect some for their own use.

The windows for the extension failed to arrive therefore work began on the construction of the raised beds, further enhancing my perception of an archaeological dig.

Fred and I left the chaos to attend the end-of-term celebrations at my old school. I had faced the inevitable and had resigned on the grounds of ill-health. I had always found leaving a teaching position difficult as the very nature of teaching demands involvement with other people and I became more involved than most. When I had left other teaching posts my sadness at leaving had always been mixed with pleasant anticipation of the next position. I had always chosen the next step and prepared my departure – now? I was the Coordinator for Science and Technology and I had been very involved with plans for the school to become a City Technology College. I had a large teaching and pastoral commitment, including A level and GCSE groups. I had

More progress and some light gardening.

been running an Information Technology course for all the staff. My departure was not planned – but no-one is indispensable. The next step – my future is so frightening I do not think about it. As I have said before, others were involved with my future requirements and my 'sell by date;' I was able to survive by refusing to think about the true situation. We left early, sadly I had no part to play any more, the school had moved on. But I had changed. I needed to concentrate on today's problems.

At the beginning of August the insurance company named the doctor of their choice. According to the legal schedule arranged by the court, exchange of all relevant documentation was due to take place on the thirteenth of August, therefore the appointment had to take place quickly. I believed that if we had a ruling from the court both sides were obliged to comply. It was years later I realized how naive, trusting and foolishly innocent this opinion was.

During August my physiotherapist went away for two weeks' holiday and gave me a list of daily exercises. Over time the number and the type of the exercises has changed but I always spend at least an hour every day exercising at home.

NHS speech therapy provision had ended when I was discharged from hospital. Sadly, my speech problems did not also discharge! I now attend a private speech therapist who makes use of a computer to aid and measure speech development. My work on the computer was followed by breathing and muscle development exercises. Some of the breathing exercises involved blowing bubbles from soap solution, party poopers and a windmill. I performed these exercises whilst using my standing frame.

A wooden standing frame is very large. A series of long leather straps, encased in sheepskin sheaths, were fixed around me, to hold me in an upright position. The removal men made interesting speculations regarding its probable use – none of them decent enough to share with you!

I travelled to my various therapies in a taxicab, sitting in my

INJURY, REHABILITATION AND INSURANCE

wheelchair looking out of the back window. This situation provided another opportunity for the speech therapy exercises. Many motorists must have questioned my sanity as they observed my facial muscle development exercises! I also performed unnecessary chewing movements on a diet of puréed food. A second videofluoroscopy confirmed there had been an improvement, however, my swallowing reflex is initiated later than is normal, therefore mouthfuls of food have to be small and eating is a lengthy process.

I was making progress and the building project advanced. The raised beds at the side of the property were capped with engineering bricks and half filled with rubble. The rubble was the product of the building work, which had caused the total collapse of one ceiling and the partial collapse of another – the rubble was very plentiful and easy to detect. Building progress was less tangible and remained harder to detect.

The windows and external doors arrived for the altered side of the property. One door was damaged and we discovered later that one window was broken. We chose units for the carer's kitchen and made arrangements for the refitting of the carpets we had brought with us into rooms on the builders' side of the screen. We ordered the much-needed wardrobes.

The sanitary ware for the new master bathroom arrived. The toilet was plumbed in position before Fred discovered we had been supplied with the wrong toilet and bidet. There were no fixing screws for the washbasin and no bath. The builders obviously could not proceed with the bathroom, they wanted to make a start on the carer's accommodation.

Our first major hitch, since we were using the shower room which was destined to be en suite in the carer's flat. The doorway into the inner hall was filled in and the bed-sitting room of the carer's flat extended. This allowed new doorways to open from the carer's bed-sitting room into the inner hall, on the builder's side of

Looking down on the collapsed ceiling.

the screen, and one into the shower room. Therefore we no longer had access to the shower room. The only bathroom, on our side of the screen, was the small, green bathroom, nicknamed 'the bathroom from Hell'.

The bathroom was too small to allow wheelchair access so I needed a considerable amount of help to enter. The carers could not manage the manoeuvre, therefore a commode joined the miscellany of items in the dining room – our temporary bedroom.

The bathroom itself – imagine a green-tiled decor with green sanitary ware. To make your imaginary picture correct every green needs to be a different shade, the sanitary ware, each piece a different vintage. The small wall tiles need to be imagined without grouting. The floor was covered with modern, cracked, cream ceramic floor tiles. There was an electric shower unit fixed on the wall above the bath, which did not work, and the toilet leaked; the leak was not easy to detect but a quick sniff would tell you something was amiss.

It may be hard to believe but our problems did not end there. The work on the carer's accommodation required moving a radiator. All the heating pipes ran under the floor of the inner hall so the floorboards were lifted creating an unusual subterranean feature. Going to the bathroom necessitated crossing the inner hall and this became quite an experience!

Several weeks later the next, but not the final, instalment of sanitary ware was delivered, but the bath remained conspicuous by its absence. The bath, like all the other sanitary ware, was designed for use by a disabled person, so the builders had no choice other than to wait for delivery.

Towards the end of August the bath finally arrived and was plumbed in position. All the rooms, including the corridor on the builders' side of the screen were painted. All the pipe work was completed ready for the change from an oil-fired boiler located in the main part of the kitchen to a gas-fired boiler housed in a cupboard in the utility section of the kitchen. The oil tank was tilted to make sure as much of the oil as was possible was used before the change of boiler was made.

The company making the units for the carer's kitchen were on strike, so I went to choose other units. The only criterion for my choice was instant availability!

To enable wheelchair entry, the steps at all the doors had to be removed. To allow paved solid surfaces to be adjacent to the bungalow walls grating, concealing drainage troughs, was placed around the bungalow. The ground sloped steeply, therefore to make the slope on the path safe for a wheelchair the path was elevated and now has a small retaining wall.

I had an encouraging session with my speech therapist who considered I was making real progress. Despite this good news I was unable to relax, constantly worried about what would happen

JULY-DECEMBER 1996

Building the ramped path.

next. One of my immediate problems was financial, as I was committed to spending £1,400 every month beyond our joint income. This was the cost of the various therapies, the taxis to take me to and from the places I visited during the week, and the care I required. The burdens caused by the building work, coupled with legal and financial worries, were almost unbearable.

The insurance company agreed to a further interim settlement but they had still not served the long overdue counter schedule of loss. The solicitor explained she was preparing to go to court to force their hand. My trusting, innocent naivete continued.

We were told by the builders they hoped to change sides on the fourth of October, so we finalized the arrangements to have the carpets, which remained rolled in the garage, fitted into the completed rooms. Friends agreed to help my husband with the move.

On Friday, 27 September we received copies of all the reports the 'other side' had commissioned, plus a copy of the long-awaited counter schedule of loss. We could not deal with them immediately, Fred went to work and I went to hydrotherapy.

Another client using the hydrotherapy pool gave me a bottle of a herbal tonic he took each day, claiming it had made a huge difference to his recovery. My husband looked at the list of contents, called it 'jungle juice' and advised me not to take it.

On Saturday, Matthew and Jay came to help tidy up the mountain of logs. I was experiencing abdominal pain and against Fred's advice I took my first dose of 'jungle juice'. I had a further dose on Sunday.

Fred and I spent a large part of the weekend responding to the documents I had received. The abdominal pain increased and the significance of what I read did not register.

We were both surprised by the number of factual errors contained in the report presented by the medical services specialist. The errors were numerous: my date of birth was wrong, by a mere twenty years, while Fred's, Kathryn's and Matthew's ages were all incorrect. The most surprising chronological mistake was the date of the accident. The report stated:

> I have calculated the life care costing for Mrs Davison up to the age of seventy as the medical reports do not suggest a reduction in life expectancy.

She appeared to have used the 'three score years and ten' quotation from the Bible as a source of fact, although the Registrar General's life expectancy tables for a woman disagree with the Bible on this point!

The report stated that I used *Fixo* to thicken drinks; I had a '*Mengel*' wheelchair; I used to teach *computer skills* in a *college*; I travelled using the *free Readybus*; I needed *micro enemas once a week*; I had *published cookery books*; and the carer accompanied me to the therapy sessions. I had considered purchasing a '*Vauxhall Caravelle*' but I had actually purchased a *VW Sharon*.

JULY-DECEMBER 1996

Fred told her I use Thixo, I had a Mangar wheelchair, I used to teach science in a comprehensive school, I had purchased a VW Shar<u>a</u>n. I have never heard of the model the report refers to:

Vauxhall Caravelle GL Plus Internal conversion . . . £22,400.00

The <u>Readibus</u> is not free, I was not accompanied to therapy sessions and I have never published cookery books. There was a further comment about the wheelchair:

The purchase of this chair would also negate the need to purchase a separate armchair as Mrs Davison would be able to change her position within the chair.

I have no idea how she considered I could do this. I have purchased a reclining chair which will go horizontal and also lifts me to a standing position to allow transfer to the wheelchair. Fred asked if she wished to see transfers when she made her one and only visit. She declined the offer. Therefore her opinion was formed as I sat in a wheelchair and she talked mainly with my husband. She made a few very brief notes.

The report contained several typing errors. The decimal point had been typed in the wrong place reducing the cost of a Mangar wheelchair tenfold. I have never heard of a Mengel wheelchair.

Mengel Freestyle Wheelchair . . . £516.72

Other examples: *spleenectomy; Dr Davison has full care of he wife and the household during the weekend.*

These errors are facts but the report went on to express an opinion about physiotherapy, hydrotherapy, aromatherapy, speech therapy and counselling. I was surprised one person had such wide-ranging qualifications and could formulate an opinion without examination.

Maybe her introduction provides the answer. All the other experts' reports began with their qualifications. This one did not.

INJURY, REHABILITATION AND INSURANCE

Instead the introduction gave a brief history of the events which culminated in an interview on Friday 10 July at 10.00 a.m.:

As scheduled I visited Mrs Davison in her home, her husband was present throughout the assessment. At a later date I received correspondence from . . . . . . [she names an employee of a named Insurance Company] enclosing further reports for my perusal and requesting that I also include in my report my opinion and the cost to date of care and money spent on personal aids and various therapies. He also asked me to comment on the Plaintiff's schedule of Damages, particularly to the item concerning the therapies envisaged in the future.

I have no way of knowing if she possessed any further qualifications other than those recorded after her name, which were RGN. DIP Counselling Medical Services Consultant. The opinion expressed in this report was treated as fact for the construction of the counter schedule of loss. Our numerous experts' reports and their own medical expert's report appeared to be ignored. All the ignored reports were compiled after a full medical examination.

Her opinion with regard to the therapies:

Physiotherapy – I would therefore recommend two sessions per week at £25 per session.

Hydrotherapy – unless this is recommended by the consultants I believe this would be an option and should be funded by the Davisons if they require it.

Massage and Aromatherapy – once again I believe this is a choice rather than a necessity and it should therefore be funded by the Davisons.

The care plan advocated in the report:

The cost of a residential live in carer would be approximately £50.00 per day for five days per week Monday to Friday, £250 per week.

JULY-DECEMBER 1996

This opinion was followed by a debate about National Insurance and bank holidays but no mention of the weekends.

The accountant's report was, in part, a response to the report written by my forensic accountant:

> I have excluded items which the defence care expert says are not required.
>
> I have not had sight of exhibit 6.
>
> I include no allowance for the cost of hydrotherapy, as I note that ...... considers that hydrotherapy is not a necessity.
>
> I have not had sight of exhibit 7.
>
> I have not had sight of exhibit 8.
>
> I have not had sight of ...... [the report written by the rehabilitation consultant].

All these documents were disclosed to the 'other side' and they explained the need for care and all the therapies. I can only guess at a reason to explain why this expert did not see them. His report continues:

> I have briefly reviewed ...... care report and have reflected her views and made certain assumptions to reach the revised table of past and future costs.

He did not share the biblical view of life expectancy. His report included care costs from the age of seventy.

The report of the quantity surveyor was a theoretical debate and arrived at a conclusion after the initial admission:

> I have never visited [our bungalow].

Therefore, he had not seen the bungalow but more importantly he had not seen me. His lack of experience in building for the disabled was exemplified by his reference to the sanitary fittings:

the normal £1,500 for a disabled suite.

I wonder what a normal, disabled person is like, presumably like me! However, their own care specialist's opinion was:

> ... the installation of a Parker Bath at a cost of £4,900.00.

His report gave various further examples of my extravagance and allowed him to come to the conclusion:

> I therefore consider approximately half the expenditure... is betterment over and above a reasonable claim under the terms of the insurance policy.

The conclusions contained in these three reports conflicted with the reports of the experts I had used but they also conflicted with their own medical expert who said:

> She has a severe left-sided paralysis and generally uses a powered wheelchair in the house. She is able to take a few steps with an assistant holding her and she requires one person for transferring. She cannot turn in bed. She requires a carer all the time. She is able to dress the top half of her body with difficulty but cannot dress the lower half. She is only able to use her right hand for eating.
>
> Mrs Davison has suffered a severe brain injury due to the traffic accident on 17.12.93. She has a combination of both physical and cognitive disabilities which in summary include impaired short term memory and concentration, significant speech and swallowing difficulties. Additionally she has profound left-sided weakness and clumsiness of the right arm. Finally she has a mixture of both anxiety and depression entirely due to the effects of the accident.
>
> She will require lifelong home care support.
>
> With respect to her life expectancy it would be reasonable to assume that this could be normal.
>
> One of her major ongoing problems is that of profound spasticity (stiffness) in the left arm and leg and there is no doubt that

spasticity can be reduced by constant physiotherapy input. It would be reasonable for this to be on a daily basis even if the duration of the treatment was no more than one hour.

My confusion was complete when I glanced at the counter schedule. My losses both past and predicted had been slashed. The views of the quantity surveyor and the care specialist had been used in the construction of the counter schedule of loss. The views of the accountant had been largely ignored, the views of their medical expert and all our reports were completely ignored.

I could ignore the pain no longer. Fred called the duty doctor; after an examination he advised me to call again if the pain persisted, or if things got worse. Things did get worse. I was very sick and at eleven o'clock in the evening Fred recalled the duty doctor. I was advised to go to hospital immediately and the doctor telephoned for an ambulance.

Once in the hospital all my usual medication was stopped and the pain was controlled by pethadin injections. Once again, I was fitted with a nasal gastric tube and a drip, and X-rays were taken. Tubes were placed in every orifice and all my normal medication was stopped. My muscle spasm increased and the advice of the consultant in charge of my rehabilitation was sought. The doctors asked my husband if I had changed my medication. When he arrived home, opening the refrigerator door he saw the opened bottle of 'jungle juice'. He rang the hospital and answered their enquiry.

The following day the pethadin injections were stopped, the nasal gastric tube was removed and I was allowed to sip water. In the afternoon I ate a yoghurt. The drip was removed and bowel function returned. A day later, the doctor could see no reason why I should not go home. I was both surprised and pleased to meet again the 'student nurse' who had supervised my eating in the rehabilitation unit. She was now a fully-trained staff nurse.

Various theories were put forward to explain my emergency admission: the 'jungle juice', the development of adhesions

INJURY, REHABILITATION AND INSURANCE

following the extensive surgery, the medication I was taking, something else as yet undetected. Although I was pleased to leave the hospital, I was both concerned and terrified the whole episode might recur.

During my stay in hospital there had been alterations in two main areas: legal and environmental.

All the reports from the 'other side' had been forwarded to our experts for their comments, the counter schedule of loss to our forensic accountant for his comments. My solicitor considered I should arrange to have another occupational care report. There were several reasons for this request: it was looking increasingly likely that the case would go to trial, and my initial report had been prepared by someone who no longer worked for the company I was using. I had acted on the advice proffered in the first report, maybe there had been a significant change.

The bungalow now enjoyed the benefits of a fully functional, quiet gas heating system. The builders had removed two sections of wall, one hole linked the kitchen and the main hall, the other hole was between the utility section of the kitchen and the main kitchen area. The dividing screen had disappeared.

The laurel hedge along the front boundary of the property had been left to grow unchecked for many years and was eight feet thick and at least twelve feet high. I am not sure 'pruning' describes the attention it received from the man Fred employed to reduce its height and spread!

The shock of the latest emergency had left its mark and I was anxious about everything. I was very concerned about the reports and the counter schedule of loss but my overriding fear was a repetition of the latest medical episode.

At the beginning of October we began to arrange affairs for the change of sides and the carpets stored in the garage were fitted into the completed rooms. I used graph paper to make scale footprints of all the furniture and together with scale drawings of the rooms I was able to decide where things would fit. I used these plans when Matthew and Jay came to help Fred move the furniture.

The impending change of sides indicated that the time had come to make a start on the kitchen. The existing kitchen cabinets had to be removed to allow the kitchen to be equipped for use by a disabled person. During the installation process Fred and I planned to use what would eventually be the carer's kitchen.

I worked with the carer to divide the kitchen contents into two groups. The items we needed were placed in the carer's kitchen. The remainder we packed into a mixture of boxes and freezer baskets. These were stored – where else but in the garage. Boxes in the garage had become a way of life!

By 11 October all the kitchen cupboards were empty and the sink unit was disconnected. The small refrigerator and the combination microwave cooker were now occupying their permanent position in the carer's kitchen. The confusion was complete when twenty tons of sand was delivered, and dumped on what remained of the gravel drive.

The 'old' kitchen furniture had been installed when the previous owner had built the first extension. The kitchen is large and it was fully fitted with both floor and wall cupboards; all the appliances had been free standing and were removed by the previous owner.

There were two floor-to-ceiling cupboards and a decorative hood unit above the place were the cooker had stood. This space had housed the refrigerator which supported the combination micro-wave cooker bought on my pre-move spending spree – I had become an expert at managing with the minimum of equipment. What you could not cook in a combination microwave oven, we did not eat. What you could not store in a very small refrigerator, I did not buy.

The units were modern and of excellent quality and included worktop illumination. It was a tragedy to remove them, but they would not allow use with a wheelchair. My sister had recently

The 'old' kitchen.

moved into an old cottage and she planned to refit the kitchen. I had so many units they would refit her complete kitchen with units to spare. This idea became the plan and we advised the builders of our intention.

My sister lives in Yorkshire and she hired a large van. My nephew came with her to help dismantle and pack the units. Kathryn and a friend provided additional assistance.

On 12 October the team to dismantle the kitchen assembled. The first task, a climb over the sand dune in the drive! The last task, hours later, again involved a climb over the dune, but this time required carrying kitchen units! It was very late in the evening when the van left for Yorkshire carrying an assortment of kitchen units, and a collection of screws and brackets that fitted somewhere!

I had always been a person that became involved with things, now my role was planning but it was not enough and I craved active involvement.

The dining room, which for months had been our bedroom and a furniture store, was now almost empty. The adjoining kitchen was a very large empty space. We placed a small table in the middle of the dining room and for the first time in seven months we were able to have a meal in a dining room. It was no consolation.

The final stage of the building work began and we changed sides. We were using the carer's kitchen and having our meals at a table in the carer's bed-sitting room. We had a bedroom to sleep in and a lounge when the builders left – what luxury!

Although progress was being made, Fred and I were both experiencing the results of fatigue and anxiety. The attempt to live in a building site, continue with my rehabilitation, manage the legal affairs and cope with my continuing ill health was too much – I had engineered an impossible situation. The building was not finished, therefore we could not employ a live-in carer. Help on a daily basis was proving to be unreliable. To add a further complication, my response to the regular enema treatment began to be erratic. I was in a lot of pain and very frightened. I responded in the usual way – the chaos around me provided the required distraction.

Distraction and chaos I had in abundance. Once again try to imagine the scene – the painter was painting the garage door, the carpenters were busy in the house and the company subcontracted to fit the double-glazed units arrived, bringing all the remaining doors and windows... they said.

Fixing the new windows and doors required the complete removal of the old ones. To facilitate this, they requested clearing or covering up the contents of the lounge and dining room. Fred helped the carer to achieve this.

This was by no means the complete picture. The oil tank and its surrounding screen of at least ten-foot-high overgrown laurel bushes were no longer needed. The builders started to remove them. Several builders were struggling with huge laurel branches, men were carrying windows, doors and frames, when a very puzzled carpet fitter arrived to measure the lounge, dining room and both halls for the new carpets. He must have thought he had arrived to witness a comedy scene. I escaped to the relative peace of the Resource Centre. I have no idea how or what he measured – the carpets but not the windows fit perfectly!

I returned to the bungalow expecting a lot to have been achieved but I was disappointed; things had happened, this much was true. The window people had fitted only four small windows. The lounge had no new windows, the furniture remained stacked in the middle. The French windows they had brought with them did not fit as they had measured the space incorrectly. In the dining room only the small window was fitted. The kitchen window was the second new window but the old outer door remained. The window in Fred's study was the third window to be fitted. The bathroom window was clear glass, although I had requested frosted glass. It seemed a minor detail to point out that the handles and ventilation grids were a different style from those installed in the other half of the bungalow.

A glance outside revealed a further problem – the fitters had broken many bricks when trying to fit the windows. The builders were fully aware of the problems and had already begun remedial work.

Fred and I continued to live, or should I be more honest and write exist, amongst the muddle and the rubble, but more was about to follow.

We employed landscape gardeners to turn my plans for the garden into reality. These plans included a garden pool. The builders arranged with the landscape gardeners to excavate the pool to the proposed depth. The soil proved to be largely rubble and was ideal for the bottom of the adjoining raised bed. Did this stony terrain explain how the original gardener's bungalow had stood for so many years on ten-inch foundations? The builders hired a digger and dumper truck. The job was nearly completed when the fated day began.

The window subcontractors arrived with the replacement doors and windows, one notable exception being the front door! Fred prepared the rooms again.

The builders were moving the excavated material to the raised bed when disaster struck. The dumper truck with its shovel full of stones tipped over trapping the driver beneath. Fortunately the shovel of the dumper truck hit the raised bed and lodged in an engineering brick. His leg was trapped and his ankle began to swell. Another builder pulled him free and assisted him into the lounge, where he sat waiting to go to hospital. His rapidly swelling ankle was covered by a large pack of frozen peas.

The relative peace of the lounge was shattered as the burglar alarm began to scream. The window fitters had removed the back door including the frame which suddenly released pressure on the pads and the alarm sounded. I was unable to reach the burglar alarm control pad from my wheelchair, and had never cancelled the alarm. Neither I, nor anyone else in the bungalow knew the code. The only person with the necessary knowledge was my husband, who was at work.

At first the alarm in the house sounded; when this was not cancelled the claxons in the roof space joined in, the noise was deafening. Many things were not working correctly but the burglar alarm certainly was!

The carer used a cordless telephone in the garden, my husband needed no explanation and peace was restored. I went to physiotherapy, the builder to the local hospital and I left the window fitters to complete the job.

There had been window problems in the past but not on this scale. A lot of the bricks around the window openings were broken, parts of the window frames were missing, the internal plaster was cracked. The French doors in the lounge were unaltered as they had measured the size incorrectly – again!

The builders had installed grating around the bungalow to allow level access. When fitting the new French doors in the dining room this point had been overlooked and there was a ledge. The ledge was so deep it was impossible for me to ride safely over. The rooms were covered with brick and fine plaster dust and the wrongly sized lounge French doors were leant against the dining-room wall.

The builders' routine had been upset by the trip to the hospital and they had omitted to order a skip. Outside there was a mountain of excess rubble excavated for the three-metre circular pool and an equally large heap of laurel branches. The old oil tank was balanced across the raised bed.

I reminded myself that I had reasoned I needed the distraction and living in a building site was preferable to owning two properties and paying for a huge bank loan – or so I had believed!

The builders used the hole, excavated for the pool, to build a giant bonfire. Using the remains of the oil in the tank all the laurel branches were burned.

Two months of 1996 remained and the chaos continued. The building work had reached a stage which allowed Kathryn to help Fred move furniture from the dining room and the lounge into my study, Fred's study and the carer's accommodation.

All the furniture had now been moved from the dining room, the carpet was rolled and placed down the centre of the room. This created a very large space which was filled the following day with the new kitchen units and most of the appliances. The very large refrigerator-freezer joined the miscellany of items in the hall.

Although it was now possible to contemplate the end, the journey remained painful and difficult. Workmen were busy everywhere. The drive was being laid, the garden pool completed, the gardeners were laying turfs and the outside lights were being fitted. The kitchen units were being assembled. This activity cleared the dining room to allow the walls and ceiling to be painted.

The French windows for the lounge were still not available but the painter agreed to leave this area and complete the rest of the room. We called upon our team of helpers to move all the lounge furniture, including the piano into the dining room and lift the lounge carpet.

Fred and I decided to pay to have the 'bathroom from Hell' attended to. The walls were stripped of tiles and the old sanitary ware removed. The source of the smell was revealed – the pipe at the back of the toilet had been leaking for some time. The floor was very wet and the plumber made a further discovery – the bath leaked. The whole room needed a new floor.

The newly painted lounge was the temporary home for the sanitary ware. This room had recently been fitted with replacement patio doors. Right this time? No such luck! Though I had to admit progress had been made. The new doors correctly fitted the opening, however, when a single door was open it was too narrow for use with a wheelchair and the handle was on the left window! I could not use it; I could not believe it.

At last the window people enlisted the help of an experienced fitter! He replaced the cracked window, the clear glass with frosted glass, and the back door and French windows in the dining room were adjusted. He started negotiations with the builders about the other problems, but a full site meeting was needed to resolve the problems with the lounge French window. The present window had four parts, two small doors and two side panels. The final solution – two doors of maximum width and one side panel. The cost of the compromise was a lack of symmetry; under the circumstances, it seemed a small price to pay.

A further compromise and the bungalow had a new front door. The company was only able to supply the carcass and a temporary solid, opaque, white infill.

To make it easier for me to leave the bungalow whilst still in my wheelchair, the front door opened outwards. The temporary infill lacked a window, so several unsuspecting visitors, including the postman and the milkman, were almost swept aside by the moving door. Fortunately the milkman learnt very quickly and we had only one near miss when full milk bottles were left in the path of the door. The infill had no letter box so I positioned a large cool box outside the door as a post box to address this problem!

The new carpet was fitted in the lounge, the team of amateur furniture movers returned and moved the furniture including the dining room furniture into the lounge. Once the dining room was cleared, the new carpet was laid in this room and the team returned to replace the furniture.

On 22 November the builders and their hut moved out, the end was in sight. I could at last begin to contemplate the next phase. I employed a case manager to oversee the arrangements to employ residential care. A primary requisite was obviously the pattern of care I required. Fred and I discussed the pattern of care we thought I needed. We both wanted to retain some time to ourselves, and realized the physical cost of this arrangement would have to be borne by Fred. We decided I required two people, each working one week on, one week off. I asked for 24-hour care from Monday morning to lunchtime on Saturday. If Fred had to be away from home the carers should be prepared to cover the complete week.

The last two months of 1996 brought some welcome personal changes. The 4th of November was a very significant day. I woke at 5.00 a.m with an intense pain in my left leg. When the pain abated I was surprised to find I was able to bend my left knee! I was now able to walk a few yards with the minimum amount of support.

I received an injection of botulinum toxin A into the gastrocnemius muscle of my left leg. This reduced the muscle spasm and my foot went flatter, but not flat, when I tried to stand.

My physiotherapist talked with me about going to Queen's Square to receive botulinum toxin A injections into my left arm. She thought this experimental technique was my best opportunity to increase mobility in my left hand.

A diet of all puréed food has little to commend it. Experimentation with food of a different texture had always resulted in coughing. I was now delighted to discover that if I took great care and only took a very small piece into my mouth I could eat soft non-puréed food. I use a selection from Greek yoghurt, homemade sauces, bottled sauce, packet sauce mixes and gravy granules to achieve the correct consistency.

Illogically, I had thought that once the kitchen was adapted I would be able to cook as I used to. I was now compelled to accept that there are numerous tasks that require two hands. I wrote in my diary:

> One dreary week follows another. I look forward to nothing, except fear things will go wrong.

Fred loathes cooking, planning meals and organizing shopping. Before the accident I had used the computer to help organize my menus and the necessary shopping list. I wondered if I could adapt this scheme to take account of my disabilities and do something, rather than feeling sorry for myself.

When compiling the booklet for dysphagia I had entered the data for the puréed recipes. I added the recipes for the dishes I could now eat. This produced a bank of many hundreds of recipes. I asked Fred to make an inventory of the contents of the cupboards and the freezers.

I had managed, by chance rather than design, to be the owner of three freezers – the new refrigerator-freezer in the kitchen, the freezer I had purchased on my pre-move shopping spree and the very old chest freezer, which, despite all the gloomy predictions, still drones and freezes. I dread to think how much electricity it requires to produce the thick layer of ice on its shiny metal internal sides but it still works.

For each freezer I entered into my computer a contents list and I constructed an even longer list for the contents of the cupboards. Each week I plan the following week's menu, amend the computer lists and compile a shopping list. After shopping I use the very long till receipt to alter the computer lists and the lists are changed after cooking items for the freezers.

I compiled a further huge list of all the items used by the household. I am told when these things need replacing. This was the beginning of a system which I have amended and elaborated with time and the live-in carers. Although I am not able to go and look, I know what is in the freezers and the cupboards. My computer lists indicate when I need to reorder.

This scheme was only part of my culinary changes. I eventually found and purchased a very large number of variously sized containers with plastic lids and an airtight seal. They are opened by pressing two levers on the lid, I discovered; to my delight, I was able to open them with one hand. I placed large blue plastic spoons – one is supplied with every tub of 'Thixo' – inside the containers and even though I am unable to pour, I am able, very slowly to dispense the contents. A blue spoonful plays a large part in my new culinary life! To identify the contents, I attached printed adhesive, plastic labels to the containers. Once the carer has filled the container I can more or less proceed independently.

Once I had found a solution to my culinary problems my attention turned to the large dining room. I soon discovered the manufacture of dining tables does not have wheelchair accessibility as one of its criteria but was fortunate to discover a copy of an Irish wake's gateleg table which did have the required features! It was large enough for the room. A coffin, which it is designed to accommodate, is lengthy. The side flaps, designed to be erected for the funeral meal, would allow my wheelchair to go under!

JULY-DECEMBER 1996

The latter part of December brought changes, some more welcome than others. The front door was finally fitted. This allowed the carpenter and the painter to complete the adjoining window. The hand rails, recommended by the physiotherapist, were fixed with brass holders to a plain painted wall, a combination which affected my double vision. I have to make sure I am holding the real rail when standing or when practising stepping. The shower rail and shower curtains were fitted in the en suite bathroom. The carpets were laid in the lobby, the carer's kitchen and the en suite bathroom.

My domestic plans and the changes needed for the school to become a Technology College reached completion at the same time. I was asked to attend an awards evening and the formal opening of the new facilities. It was with very mixed emotions that I helped the local MP cut the ribbon and declare the Technology and Science suites open.

I was delighted to see the fruition of the plans I had helped to start. My personal plans had not included my retirement, riding in a wheelchair that required lifting up and down the numerous steps, or the physical and mental damage I had endured since the accident. The evening passed in a blur and I left the school for the last time.

The 9th of December proved to be a very eventful day. The long silence from the insurer's solicitors was broken with an unexpected 'out of court offer'.

The offer was lower than the insurer's own accountant had estimated I needed. It was considerably lower than the amount calculated by my forensic accountant. The offer was a total amount, nothing had been awarded for pain and suffering and nothing for loss of interest.

I had twenty-one days, which included Christmas and the New Year holidays to decide what to do. Fred and I were told the timing of the offer is referred to as the 'Christmas manoeuvre'. It is used to catch the plaintiff at a time when the legal profession are on holiday and are therefore unable to give advice. Its attraction – it facilitates completion prior to the New Year.

To make arriving at any decision more difficult there was a legal battle concerning the calculation of future losses for personal injury. The dispute centred around the way monies are invested. There is obviously a greater reward if more is risked, but equally there could be a greater loss. Obviously the method of investment played a large part in deciding the size of the settlement required. The insurance company favoured a smaller settlement, but taking greater risks with the investment.

The *Wells* v. *Wells* appeal had been resolved in favour of the insurance company, substantially reducing the amount of the Wells' award. This ruling was to go the House of Lords. However, I would be obliged to adhere to the legal precedent set by this appeal, because my case was to be heard before the *Wells* v. *Wells* case was decided by the House of Lords.

I had much to think about including the third anniversary of the accident. I escaped the thinking and used the computer to write my Christmas letter. As I struggled with the task I wondered if there was anything that could be done to increase the movements I could make with my left hand. Although I recorded this thought in my diary, my cognitive skills and use of language were such that I did not pursue it. The idea remained an entry in my diary and a suggestion made by the physiotherapist.

I had neither the knowledge nor the skills to solve the problems I faced, nor was I able to articulate them. I overheard a client talking at the Resource Centre. He said he had stopped looking forward to things – I knew exactly what he meant. I felt trapped, with a series of different carers; I was reluctant to get involved with anything. I was very concerned about the legal affairs, not for the first time, nor would it be the last; I understood why suicide rates are high in patients with head injuries! I had too many balls to juggle and could not cope with reality. Would accepting the offered settlement bring relief?

These thoughts resulted in the usual sleepless night. I had grown accustomed to waking up regularly, but no sleep at all is entirely different. I spent the night thinking. In the morning I had made several decisions, the most significant being that I had decided to write to my solicitor. I wished to hear the views of the QC but I had decided to reject the offer.

Once I had written the letter, I felt a tremendous sense of relief. There was a Christmas party at the physiotherapy clinic so I decided to go in my wheelchair decorated like a Christmas tree. This idea required covering me, wearing a green jumper and brown trousers, and the wheelchair with tinsel and baubles. Kathryn came for the evening to turn my idea into reality.

As the year drew to a close my physiotherapist told me I should aim to walk a few steps the following year. Although I made this achievement my New Year's resolution, I was unaware that the events of the following year would conspire to make this impossible.

CHAPTER XI

January-February 1997

The new year began. I was unaware that I was involved with events that would determine the rest of my life. In oblivion I persisted with my feeble attempts to make the house more comfortable. Using a combination of the curtains we had brought from the Reading house, with those we had inherited from the previous owners I was able to hang 'something' at all the windows. The curtains did not all meet when drawn across, nor were they all the correct length, nor did they complement the furniture in the room, but there were curtains at all the windows.

Fred and I set ourselves the task of unpacking one of the innumerable stored boxes per day. The target changed when we discovered that field mice were also using the garage, but not for storage. One enterprising mouse had plucked the tufts from a wool rug to make her nest, another used packing material to construct an equally comfortable home. The bungalow's other residents made unique contributions to our daily life, and deer regularly ate the new shoots from a variety of plants. A male pheasant tapped on the French window to get Fred's attention and then followed him to the garage to collect his peanuts! There was a daily competition between jays, magpies, pigeons, squirrels and a variety of small birds for any food we placed on the bird table. Needless to say the squirrels always won and the others had to be satisfied with the scraps they left, if they left any!

The new bedroom furniture was delivered. One wardrobe door

was damaged so it was returned to the shop. The automatic front-door opener was fitted; it responds to a remote control device held by me. Or to be honest, it would have responded in this way if they could have located the missing part.

Towards the end of February the missing part of the door opener was located and Matthew and Jay came once again to move furniture. They also removed the remaining boxes from the garage away from the mice and we experienced our first bad storm. The wind lashed the rain against the French windows and formed two large puddles on the new carpets – a large pool in the lounge but an even larger one in the dining room.

Fred examined the windows and discovered each window had three drainage holes, designed to drain excess water to the outside, a point that had failed to register with the fitter, presumably not the experienced one. Our drainage holes drained inside onto the carpet! Very efficient they were too!

To prevent a recurrence the builder draped very large sheets of blue plastic over the whole windows. Less than two months before I had wanted something to hang at the windows, however, I was thinking about the inside surface – and not blue plastic over the entire outer surface! It came as no surprise when we learned the window people did not want to return. Instead, they sent a diagram to the builder asking him to fill the existing holes and drill three additional holes to drain the excess water outside.

I was using the standing frame when I first became aware of the increasing size of my abdomen. I wrongly attributed this increase to a lack of exercise. My physiotherapist was concerned about my general health and advised me to consult my GP. This was sound advice, but I had no way of getting to the medical centre, two miles away from my home. I did not think my condition required a home visit, so I foolishly did nothing.

There was agreement that the trial should be heard at the High Court in London. On the very last day in February a meeting took

INJURY, REHABILITATION AND INSURANCE

place at the bungalow between the QC, his junior, my solicitor, Fred and I.

Although I was making little progress with my legal battle, I was making progress in other areas. I regularly used software designed to improve cognitive skills; I was improving. More physiotherapy had brought rewards and I was able to crawl a few yards.

As soon as the rooms for the carer were completed we advertised for two people to share the job of providing the care I needed. Fred and I made sure everything was arranged in the carer's accommodation and we took delivery of the converted Volkswagen Sharan.

The builders had removed their sign from outside the house. It had become a landmark over the past months, one we used when we gave directions to people wanting to find the bungalow, a direction we could not use when we held the interviews for the live-in carer position. We were very lucky to appoint two people to share the job.

In the middle of February the new care regime commenced. The taxi driver showed both carers the various routes he took to the different venues. My husband supplemented their knowledge with the routes in Reading.

On the last occasion I planned to go to physiotherapy with the taxi driver I was suffering acute abdominal pain, but I was determined to go, a decision that was reinforced when the taxi driver arrived in full chauffeur's dress driving a very large white limousine.

CHAPTER XII

March-April 1997

The builders persuaded the window fitters to attend to the French windows. I am not sure what form the persuasion took, but it worked and the windows received yet more attention.

The furniture store delivered and fixed in place the new wardrobe doors. Fred had used the wardrobe without doors for so long it was strange to see them. The wardrobe had other strange features – six bumps in the veneer with screws poking through two of them. The hinges were supposed to be fixed to the side panels with small screws and to the door with large screws. Unfortunately, this point was not appreciated by the delivery men. Such confidence had they in their assembly skills, they failed to check their work as they proceeded. Hence the six bumps! The store agreed we needed to have the whole wardrobe replaced! Was this once again the work of an inexperienced fitter, or just a further example of our lack of luck with doors, be they wood or glass or fitted with an opening device?

I now enjoyed greater freedom and at last I had an appointment to see the doctor. He thought the abdominal pain might have been caused by the daily medication I required, so he altered my prescription. Despite this change on 5 March I had a very disturbed night, and at five o'clock the following morning I was very sick. The duty doctor thought I had an intestinal blockage and telephoned for the ambulance.

I recalled the last time I had made the same journey. The feeling of déjà vu was reinforced when I went to the same surgical ward, where the doctor arranged for a series of X-rays to aid diagnosis.

I remained laying on the bed waiting for the porters. On arrival they asked me to hop off the bed onto the wheelchair and they would take me for an X-ray of my thorax. I explained I was unable to hop onto the chair and maybe I needed an abdominal X-ray. They left to seek advice. In their absence I was seen by the anaesthetist who would be officiating at the planned operation. The preoperative preparations caused my abdomen to begin to regain its normal size.

When the porters returned with a trolley, the abdominal X-rays confirmed that things were returning to their normal size. The plans for the operation were abandoned, I was allowed to drink and my large intestine began to work. Later in the day I was allowed to eat; if I was not sick and the pain did not return I could go home. Twenty-four hours later I was delighted to be going home but was concerned the underlying problem had not been resolved.

I had relied on phosphate enemas for three years; when we lived in Reading I had seen a medical consultant and twice I had been admitted to a surgical ward, there seemed to be no reason why the medication I was taking should have this effect. I had not taken any more 'jungle juice'. Another client at the physiotherapy clinic was using a dietary regime recommended by Stoke Mandeville Hospital. I wondered if I should seek a solution there so Stoke Mandeville Hospital was contacted by telephone and I requested an appointment through my GP. I began to use their dietary regime.

Towards the end of March I experienced spasmodic results with the measures I was taking to alleviate the intestinal problems. I ended the month, as I had begun it, in acute abdominal pain.

I was suffering the additional discomfort of a mouth ulcer. When the glands in my neck became enlarged I saw the doctor. I was feeling so ill, the entry in my diary records my desperate state:

> I went to bed and hoped I did not wake in the morning.

MARCH-APRIL 1997

I lived to see another day and despite all the abdominal problems my stamina had improved and my physiotherapist agreed to some extra sessions. The clinic had recruited more staff which included a neurophysiotherapist. When the middle of April approached I had my first session with the neurophysiotherapist. I could walk across the gymnasium with the therapist holding the back waistband of my trousers. Although I was suffering acute abdominal pain, I was making progress.

After a further consultation with the doctor in which he could find nothing wrong I decided I was making a fuss and I attended the planned physiotherapy session.

During the evening I began to be very sick. Once more I was admitted into hospital. I was on the same surgical ward but now the night staffing problems were more acute. I was not able to move when in bed and after being sick I rang for assistance. I laid in vomit – three times I rang the bell, and three times I saw the light on the wall go out indicating the bell had been cancelled. During this time, thirty very long minutes, I made a decision: I would move to a private hospital where the staffing problems would not be so acute.

The surgeon said the intestinal problems had gone on long enough, the underlying cause had to be discovered. Barium was inserted to allow X-rays of the large intestine to be taken. I was following the twice-daily enema regime to remove the barium when two days later I was transferred to a private hospital.

The change of hospital did not require a change of surgeon. The surgeon explained that he thought there was a kink in the intestine and that I needed an operation. I signed the consent form. I needed a more extensive operation than he had anticipated. The whole of the large intestine was enormously swollen and inflamed, which explained the increasing size of my abdomen and the pain. The major part of the large intestine, the caecum and appendix were all removed and the end of the small intestine was joined to

INJURY, REHABILITATION AND INSURANCE

the rectum. I had an epidural device fitted to my back which delivered a regular supply of morphine.

The month ended in a blur of pain. My intestines resisted all attempts to make them begin to work.

CHAPTER XIII

May - October 1997

Relentlessly the latest crisis continued. I started to vomit intestinal secretions and had a chest infection. Fred recalled the Cambridge experiences, as once again he was approached by a surgeon who told him of his concern. Kathleen came down from Yorkshire. I was really frightened and my acting ability deserted me for a time, long enough to ascertain Kathleen would stay with my family for as long as she was needed. We did not speak of death, we did not need to, it was understood.

I can remember laying under the X-ray machine, while in an adjacent small room the medical team organized a series of plates which would allow them to investigate the problem. The surgeon considered I needed another operation. The anaesthetist was concerned about my chest infection. He said, unless a ventilator was near at hand and an intensive care bed available, it was too dangerous to proceed.

Over the next hours, using a combination of exercises, oxygen and inhalers, I worked with the physiotherapist in an attempt to clear my chest. The hospital did not have intensive care facilities, therefore I was transferred when an operating theatre and an intensive care bed became available locally.

The plan of action devised by the medical team in that small room had not considered the effect of an accident by a hospital porter. He had fallen down a flight of steps which caused a bone to perforate a major artery. He required an emergency operation so he took the space reserved for my operation.

I continued to be extremely sick and very frightened. I was fitted with a nasal gastric tube and late in the evening the operation was successfully performed. The operation gave me an ileostomy, a gastrostomy and a direct line into a major blood vessel.

The following account is an attempt to explain the need for and the outcome of the two operations. The next few paragraphs can be omitted by those readers who have no desire to further their medical knowledge.

The alimentary canal is a long tube extending from the mouth to the anus. There are different regions of this tube dedicated to perform certain tasks. The function of the entire canal is the breakdown of food into a soluble form. Soluble food can be absorbed and transported by the blood system around the entire body. What remains in the tube after digestion is eliminated from the body.

Digestion starts with the mechanical breakdown of the food by the teeth; chemical, enzyme-controlled breakdown also starts in the mouth and continues in the stomach and throughout the small intestine. The process of chemical breakdown occurs in a very watery environment, the fluid and enzymes are released from glands associated with the alimentary canal.

Each region of the tube has a structure ideally suited to its particular function. The first part of this tube, the oesophagus enlarges to form the stomach, a muscular sac with circular muscles at both ends. When these muscles contract they confine the food in the stomach. The food is retained in the stomach for several hours, it is churned and chemically digested. Periodically, the lower sphincter muscle relaxes and the contents leave gradually and move into the small intestine. The small intestine, twenty-two feet long, has finger-like structures called villi, located on the internal folds. These three features increase the surface area, to aid the release of fluid and enzymes to break down the food and the absorption of the soluble food. The gut contents are moved down the tract by muscular contractions. At the end of the small intestine they are pushed into the large intestine. The caecum and appendix are also found at this junction. The excess fluid is re-absorbed by the first part of the large intestine, the colon. The waste is stored in the final part, the rectum and is periodically expelled from the body.

Which is a very elaborate way of saying food goes in one end, soluble food is absorbed by the blood stream and the waste is expelled at the other end.

What went wrong? Initially the problem was thought to be that the tube was blocked somewhere. The waste could not leave therefore more food could not go down the tube. The upper sphincter muscle of the stomach relaxed and I was sick. Put very crudely what could not go down the tube went up the tube.

There is a further entrance into the digestive tract. At the back of the throat four openings converge: the nasal passage, the passage from the mouth, the oesophagus and the trachea which takes air into the lungs. The trachea is kept open by incomplete rings of cartilage, the oesophagus is squashed between the backbone and the trachea, food is pushed down the oesophagus. This arrangement allows you to breathe all the time. Problems arise every time you swallow, as the food and saliva must go down the squashed oesophagus not the open trachea. The disaster of choking is prevented by the epiglottis, which is the hinged lid of the trachea. When swallowing it closes over the trachea and the ball of food or saliva enters the oesophagus. If your epiglottis is not in position the ball of food goes the wrong way – down the trachea. Coughing causes the ball of food to rise up the trachea to the throat and it then goes the right way, down the oesophagus.

This junction can be utilized when the oral intake of food is impossible, as it was in Cambridge or now, to remove excess intestinal secretions. A tube runs up the nose, down the nasal passage and enters the throat. At the junction it is directed into the oesophagus and enters the stomach, the so-called nasal gastric tube.

The first operation identified and removed any blockage. My caecum, appendix and colon were also removed – the parts they play in the digestive process I could no longer perform. I would never suffer from appendicitis but I could not re-absorb the excess fluid.

There was no blockage and yet my intestines refused to expel the waste. The intestinal problems were more extensive than was at first thought. The intestinal fluid built up, both sphincters of the stomach opened and I repeatedly expelled the intestinal fluid.

My alimentary canal was not working, therefore soluble food needed to be taken to the blood system by another route. I needed a direct line, which is a tube running into a major blood vessel.

I also needed stoma or holes to provide other ways into and out of the alimentary canal. The operation gave me a gastrostomy into the stomach and an ileostomy out of the small intestine. The direct line was established before I left the intensive care unit and a new epidural was fitted to maintain the regular supply of morphine.

My stay in the intensive care unit remains a blur. I can remember the pain and my overriding ambition to go back to the other hospital. In my muddled brain I equated leaving the intensive care unit with recovery.

I can remember little of the next days. I made the return journey. I know regular blood tests were required to monitor the effects of the direct line and there was a need to try to use my alimentary canal as soon as possible.

The two stoma allowed gradual use, and when feeding via the gastrostoma was established, the direct line was removed. Before the gastrostoma could be closed I had to demonstrate I could eat puréed food. This stage was reached before I was discharged. The ileostomy allowed the small intestine to be used but not the last part of the canal. The closure of the ileostomy was planned for a time after discharge.

A team of nurses holding the various tubes, bags and the epidural pump were required to allow me to work with the physiotherapist. The removal of the urinary catheter allowed me to dispense with the help of one of the nurses.

Both of my carers came to receive instructions from the stoma nurse. It was fortunate that both of them had experience with the care required by a person with a colostomy, and they quickly learned how to deal with the more complex demands of an ileostomy.

Their visit coincided with the first entry into my diary for some time. Although the entry was very brief its presence indicated a return to normality. If my life can ever be described as normal!

I was in hospital when I had my first experience of dealing with the effects of a leakage from the ileostomy pouch. The ileostomy pouch collects the liquid waste from the small intestine. The pouch is held in place with an adhesive flange and emptied regularly during the day. A leakage during the night is most unpleasant, especially so, because I am unable to change my position in bed.

Physically I was making slow progress, although I could only take two steps with a great deal of help from the physiotherapist and the full team – it was two steps.

Mentally? The nurses, consultants and all the staff were so cheerful and positive I did not consider the seriousness of my situation or the difficulties I was about to encounter. I had but one thought, I was going home. I was discharged at five o'clock on 22 May. Another long stay in hospital came to an end.

In the hospital I had slept on a Nimbus air mattress. Once at home, I needed only one night to discover I was experiencing far too much pain to rest without one. Fred arranged the purchase and a mattress was delivered the following day.

Most patients go to the chemist shop with a prescription and leave with a little package. The carers go weekly and literally come away with a carrier bag. My GP was concerned about the gastric effects of the long-term use of the pain-relieving medication. The medical staff at the hospital had expressed concern about my low body weight. There was now a need for additional medication and enriched drinks, aptly called 'Build Up'. I am not sure who or what derives the greatest benefit, me or the biceps of the carers struggling with the ever-increasing weight of the carrier bag!

Once the initial difficult period passed, both carers agreed to work together to look after me during the day, with one remaining as usual in the evening. This arrangement enabled my husband to go back to work. I always wake regularly during the night, but this restlessness was now accompanied by frequent leaks from the ileostomy pouch. Each leakage inevitably required a change of bedding and I needed a change of clothing. I could not move out of the bed without a great deal of assistance, however, on some occasions Fred was able to manage all this by himself. The only evidence of the disturbed night was the mound of washing in the kitchen the following morning. At other times Fred had to wake the carer for assistance. In an attempt to prevent these leakages the pouch was emptied every morning at two o'clock.

As was rapidly become the norm I had further problems. My financial state required another interim settlement. The 'other side' made payment dependent on me agreeing to see their medical expert. I was told by my solicitor that their request was irregular, but I agreed to the visit as I had nothing to hide. Were the 'other side' concerned about me, or were they again considering my sell-by date? Time would tell.

On 4 June I celebrated my birthday with a return to physiotherapy. Both carers came with me and they bought a selection of cakes to mark the occasion. Ever since my discharge from hospital I had enjoyed my breakfast in bed and a rest in the afternoon. I decided the time had come 'to get a grip' and these indulgences I dispensed with.

Once again I could not cope with my reality and I turned my attention to domestic matters. These included the collection of samples of curtaining for the lounge, hall and our bedroom and to the hunt for an electric pump to raise water from the old garden well.

The well is a testament to the skills of the workmen of a bygone age. My husband used a plumb line to ascertain its depth. It is at least twenty-five feet deep with a circular brick construction. The pipe which used to take water to the hand pump in the kitchen has been retained. I was told that the construction of brick wells starts from the top – the method of construction, like the source of the water, is a mystery to me.

The back garden bore the scars of tree removal and the laying of the new drains so work began to clear the stones. No sooner had one layer of stones been removed then the next downpour brought a fresh supply to the surface. I think the supply of stones was infinite. The attempt was eventually abandoned, topsoil was spread over the ground and turf was laid.

The 1997 Wimbledon's Tennis Open Championship's loss was our gain and in torrential rain the gardeners were able to lay turf. Although they were soaked, the wet weather was enjoyed by their spaniel dog! The bad weather continued and the new turf benefited from the rain. There was certainly no need to keep them damp!

I was trying desperately to become involved with something I could influence, in order to stop myself from worrying about those I could not. These were the ever-present concerns about the legal situation and my vision. Additionally, despite the 2.00 a.m. precaution the ileostomy pouch continued to leak. I was also convinced that the need for a second emergency operation meant that the ileostomy was a permanent feature; I did not share my views with anyone else.

INJURY, REHABILITATION AND INSURANCE

A sequence of intestinal X-rays on 23 June confirmed my privately-held suspicions – there appeared to be a risk to the closure of the stoma. The intestinal damage was more extensive than had first been thought. The carers and Fred were shocked by the prognosis, while the surgeon wanted me to seek a second opinion. He was able to confirm that the operations had had no long-term effects on life expectancy.

The following week I had two visitors – the doctor representing the 'other side' and the stoma nurse. Time would tell the significance of the first visit, the second visitor could offer no further help.

Fred was exhausted and he arranged to take annual leave to read the draft of a PhD thesis and to tidy up all the legal documentation I had acquired. He was becoming increasingly frustrated and annoyed by the amount of his time he had to devote to my legal battle. Because 'a battle' was how it now felt to both of us.

I had thought that insurance was meant to provide the finances to allow the constraints caused by an accident to be minimized. Maybe the present battle was to assess the nature of these constraints. Although I tried to adopt coping strategies, the tension was taking its toll and I frequently had a headache. I knew I could not endure much more.

For several weeks I had followed the consultant's recommendation for daily physiotherapy. Sunday was my only free day. I was tired, frustrated and worried. What was the point of going on? Would I ever be better? What would better be like? However, my equilibrium was restored by an event at hydrotherapy where the session was taken by a recently qualified physiotherapist. As a student she had spent her work experience on the rehabilitation unit when I was a patient, and so I was delighted she observed significant improvements. I began to put things back into perspective. I realized daily physiotherapy and the exercise regime did work, so I approached the exercises with renewed vigour.

MAY-OCTOBER 1997

The physiotherapist's observation triggered a more positive frame of mind. I had inherited an old sundial face from my parents' home and I arranged to have a local stonemason build a stand. We also bought an oak settle for the hall. My positive frames of mind are always expensive!

This one was destined to be short lived – following another eventful night with the ileostomy pouch, I sank further into depression and desperation.

Help for the intestinal problems came from an unexpected source. My physiotherapist had another client with an ileostomy, who lived for part of the year in France. When she was in England she saw a stoma nurse in Dorset whom she described as brilliant. Several telephone calls were required, including one to France, before an appointment was arranged with the Dorset stoma nurse. This visit marked the beginning of my recovery. There is a system which prevents overnight leaks from the pouch, or to be more exact, the expertise of this nurse, a fellow sufferer, was able to devise one. I left with a small library of literature. I have faced many problems but none, fingers crossed, that this stoma nurse has not been able to solve. After this visit Fred and I had our first undisturbed night for three months.

A series of events brought August to a dramatic conclusion – I had my first fall and subpoenas were served on the expert witnesses. The most dramatic and tragic event was not personal but the death of Diana Princess of Wales in a car accident, and the early part of the next month brought incredible scenes of public grief at the funeral. This event provided me with an opportunity to put my own problems into perspective.

The following week I had an appointment with a consultant in Oxford, who had agreed to provide the second opinion. He shared the forebodings concerning the closure of the stoma and offered me a series of tests to confirm his opinion. My mental argument took the following path: if the stoma was successfully closed, which seemed unlikely – nothing could be done to remove the effects of the lack of a colon, which is the production of large amounts of watery waste – I could not move independently, so I would need to have a carer with me during the night to assist me to the bathroom. The implications for the provision of this care and for yet another change in my lifestyle seemed enormous, so I declined the tests. The tests could not alleviate the situation. I knew from bitter experience confirmation did not bring relief. Foolishly, I did not consider the legal implications nor any effect it may have for the recruitment of carers in the future.

I did not want my already constrained life to be constrained further. As a result of hemiplegia I am unable to deal with any aspect of ileostomy care, an additional responsibility for the carers. Fred wondered what type of future we had. I questioned the whole of my rehabilitation and tried once again to analyse the position. Should I try to come to terms with life as it was then? Hard work had brought about changes in my speech; I could now eat a diet of soft food; there was no longer a need to purée everything; I needed less thickener in my drinks; physiotherapy, hydrotherapy and aromatherapy were bringing changes to my hemiplegia and spasticity and they definitely reduced the pain. This analysis haunts me, so on this occasion I concluded, yes of course it was worth trying. I picked up the juggling balls and continued with the performance. I tried to concentrate on what had happened and what might happen if I continued to work hard.

Since the onset of the latest set of intestinal problems I had not been able to attend the Resource Centre. The staff could see no insurmountable difficulties to my return, and several days after the Oxford visit I had my first day back. I made arrangements to resume the aromatherapy massage. By lunchtime I was settled back into the old routine, felt the benefit of the massage and I was looking forward to playing 'Scrabble'. I played with an acquaintance whom I first met as a 'Scrabble' opponent when we were both patients in the Rehabilitation Unit.

Double vision and frequent headaches prompted me to seek further help. I spent the latter part of the month adjusting to the findings of an orthoptic eye test. My eyes are misaligned both horizontally and vertically, therefore prisms which can correct misalignment in one plane can not be used.

Everything appears flat and the same distance away. Fred had screamed in horror as I approached a step which I did not see as I thought it was flat! The carer had rescued me from the top of a flight of steps and pedestrians scatter as I approach in my power chair! Venturing to a strange place is too dangerous for both me and the general public; going anywhere on my own is a dangerous impossibility.

I was not the only person with eye problems. One of the carers woke to see something she described as puffs of smoke in one eye. She was due to go on three weeks' holiday but before embarking on the vacation she visited the hospital. There she learned that the vitreous humour had pulled away from the retina. When she returned from her holiday, she had further eye problems and could not drive.

During her vacation I had relied on the goodwill of the other carer and Fred, but the care situation was reaching breaking point. Fred was exhausted. I was very vulnerable with only two people involved with the care, and I reluctantly accepted that another consequence of the accident was the requirement to have 24-hour cover seven days a week.

The headaches I was suffering had become a regular occurrence. I wondered if I was dehydrated. Could it be the effects of misaligned eyes? Too many balls to juggle? I increased my fluid intake and the number of occasions when I wore my glasses. The juggling balls remained, and the headaches remained.

According to a well-known proverb, problems come in threes; I am sure that whoever was responsible for my allocation was very bad at arithmetic! An infected big toe was added to my quota – standing during the physiotherapy sessions was difficult. The progress I had made and the additional confidence I had gained were lost. To make things more complex, both my physiotherapists now had additional work away from the clinic. If they could not treat me I was seen by another therapist. Despite the involvement of three people, the organization of the facilities and the sessions proved to be very difficult.

My toe had not responded to the treatment. During physiotherapy sessions I tried to work through the pain. The physiotherapist was concerned and suggested using a chiropodist.

CHAPTER XIV

November 1997-January 1998

Legal requirements, care arrangements, physiotherapy, hemiplegia and ill health all made their diverse demands. Their combined effect was to make me feel like a juggler who was trying to rise on the descending escalator. I was attempting the impossible.

In order to rationalize the physiotherapy situation, I started to attend a different physiotherapy centre and I increased the number of hydrotherapy sessions. The physiotherapy sessions were augmented with an additional daily programme of exercises planned by the therapist. The idea of converting a section of the garage to make a 'gymnasium' was born. I needed resolution of the insurance claim before I could make a start on the project. For the present the bed, the cork mat from the bathroom and the bars in the hall had to suffice.

To try to reduce the spasticity of the gastrocnemius muscle and to allow my left foot to go flat on the floor, I received a further botulinum toxin A injection into the muscle. When I consulted an orthopaedic surgeon about my spastic left hand, he required to manipulate the hand before he could advise on further treatment. The manipulation was planned for the beginning of January.

I had one more item to add to my medical concerns. The physiotherapist observed I did not bend my left leg in supported walking. He asked me to face the wall bars and, holding the bars, to bend my left leg towards my bottom. I was unable to do it unless I could see my leg as I had no idea where it was in space. I was unable to say whether it was bent or straight.

INJURY, REHABILITATION AND INSURANCE

Despite this difficulty the new exercise regime was making obvious improvements. I began to try and climb the wide tiled steps out of the hydrotherapy pool using a metal railing for support. My aim was to enter and leave the pool without the use of the hoist. I can now do this.

The physiotherapist who investigated the bending of my left leg still uses electrical impulses from a Faraday machine to stimulate activity. I was already beginning to respond to the treatment and on 21 January I woke in intense pain. When the pain in my leg abated I had undergone another sudden and dramatic change – the leg was easier to bend. The treatment is still continuing but a two-pound weight is now attached to my leg! I soon discovered that success with a physiotherapy exercise is quickly followed by a movement of the goalposts!

The medical problems were insignificant compared with the problems associated with my care requirements. I was very vulnerable with only two carers and I knew the burden of my care at the weekends was an impossibly heavy load for Fred to carry. I needed to look for a third person to do the weekend duties.

Fred was aware, when he attended a residential meeting, that there were no applicants for the weekend position. The effects of this situation became academic when he returned home and the carer experiencing eye problems gave me the required one week's notice.

With the proximity of the Christmas holidays, the case manager advised waiting until the New Year to seek a replacement. Meanwhile, she arranged live-in help for the Christmas period. The other carer agreed to a daily care routine with Fred providing care every night and all the weekends and also for the weeks before and after Christmas. He reluctantly cancelled a three-day meeting which required him being away from home. Increasingly he said, 'What can go wrong, will go wrong.' This statement was always accompanied, by the now familiar curse upon the cause of our problems, as he saw it. When Fred returned to work he was worn out with the activities over his so-called Christmas holiday.

The position of carer was advertised and I was successful. I appointed a person to work for one full week, every other week. The case manager knew of a third person who was prepared to cover the remaining days, giving me 24-hour cover seven days a week.

The new appointee was shortly due to have a holiday, the timing of which coincided with my court case, but as the existing carer had agreed to accompany me to the trial, her holiday presented no insurmountable problems. She agreed to work alongside the existing carer for part of the following week and visited the different venues. Her introduction to the new job was at an unusual time to say the very least.

Throughout this period the legal situation had become increasingly complex. During November I learned that my solicitor was pregnant and was going to leave her present position. The latter part of the month was dominated by the preparation of the revised schedule of loss, which was a baptism of fire for my new solicitor. Every spare moment I had was devoted to the completion of the document.

On Christmas Eve I received a telephone call informing me that the 'other side' had made an improved offer. The money had been paid into court and therefore the clock had started ticking. I had to respond within three weeks which included the Christmas and the New Year periods – the Christmas manoeuvre again! My son, with his accountancy background, agreed to spend time with me to assess the offer.

The New Year began. I was concerned when I contemplated the past year and worried about what the next year would bring. The trial was only weeks away and an offer had been made. I could end part of the present misery by accepting the offer, but would this action lead to future misery? Would I be able to pay for all the care

INJURY, REHABILITATION AND INSURANCE

which recent experience had confirmed I needed? Would I be able to pay for all the therapies which time had indicated I needed? If I did not have all the therapies, I would not be able to control the pain. Was my life to consist of pain, care, therapies and nothing else? The driver had admitted liability and he had pleaded guilty to careless driving. What obligations did the insurance company have? What was the status of the schedule of loss, our reports and their reports?

Most of the 'other side's' documents, relied on the opinion of the care services consultant, opinion which was formed without a medical examination. She was the only person from the 'other side' who had seen me, except for their medical expert. His first report came to the same conclusions as our reports, disagreeing with their care services consultant, but his first report had been ignored. Why had the 'other side' not disclosed the report they themselves had requested? Would the insurance company carry on believing a report concerning the suitability of a property for a disabled person, written without seeing me to ascertain the nature of my disabilities, or the property to assess its suitability? I came to no conclusion.

With my son's help and analysis I was able to work through the likely expenditure for the future. These calculations strengthened my resolve to reject the offer. Both my son and husband counselled caution. They argued that only the QC would know what was possible. I decided to write to the solicitor outlining my views.

As arranged I was admitted into hospital for the hand manipulation. When under the influence of the anaesthetic the surgeon bound my fingers into a bent position, while a splint held my wrist straight. Apparently I present an odd spastic pattern, my wrist is flexed and my fingers are extended; the more normal pattern is for all joints to be flexed. The surgeon asked me to keep the bandaging in place for as long as I could tolerate the pain.

As I lay, once more, in a recovery room of an operating theatre events clarified in my mind and the enormity of the whole affair registered with me. I decided to write a further letter to the solicitor. Apart from attending physiotherapy wearing the splint, I spent the following day drafting the letter. I removed the bandage in the evening, the hand was red and swollen and there was a large blister on the bone at my wrist.

The latest offer had an accompanying statement which told me if the case went to trial the 'other side' would question me about liability. This seemed illogical as they had stated to the court that the driver accepted liability. Their client had pleaded guilty to and had been charged with careless driving. I was perplexed. My solicitor could not understand their reasoning and asked for an explanation. It seemed yet another tactic to put pressure on me. It was working!

I had too many things to think about, too many 'balls' to juggle. My acting ability was put to good use. I managed, I think, to portray to the casual observer calm and control but my true feelings were expressed by the following entry in my diary:

> I feel confused, depressed and very lonely. The situation is so complex, it is difficult to talk it through with anyone, difficult to know where to begin. I am anxious about everything. I miss talking to someone who is not directly involved with the whole affair.

I was not capable of conversation. Another effect of the brain injury is that I am not able to cry. I could not understand the actions of the 'other side' and the legal wrangling continued as the trial approached.

I received the final copy of the revised schedule of loss, which was compiled according to the legal precedent set by the *Wells* v. *Wells* case. The solicitor served it on the 'other side' and sent a copy to the QC. The QC's advice was to reject the latest offer.

According to litigation procedure, I understood the 'other side' was allowed two weeks, after receipt of the revised schedule of loss,

INJURY, REHABILITATION AND INSURANCE

to produce a revised counter schedule. The schedule was served on 9 January, so my solicitor expected to receive the counter schedule in advance of a pre-trial meeting with the QC arranged for 26 January.

The latest offer was formally rejected on 12 January, the same day I saw the orthopaedic surgeon to hear the results of the manipulation. He confirmed that I should pursue the muscular injections of botulinum toxin A and only resort to an operation to make Z-cuts in the tendons if the injections failed. Sadly, the London doctor I planned to consult about further botulinum toxin A injections had recently emigrated. I am still trying to pursue a solution.

I bought a new computer and I spent the next weeks transferring all the files from my old computer, which provided a welcome distraction. I did not allow my mind to wander.

The QC requested a breakdown of the care costs for the last year. I added the information to explain why these figures could not be used to represent a typical year. At least I hoped not!

The 23rd of January marked what I hoped would be the beginning of the last phase of the legal 'war'. Battle commenced with another offer, although there was still no counter schedule, but again there was an accompanying message. More pressure? The message did not refer to liability but instead informed me that I had to respond by 4.00 p.m. on 29 January or the offer would be withdrawn and the judge would be made aware of this offer.

I was in a turmoil, I could not sleep, I had a persistent headache and the same old questions buzzed through my mind, but they were joined by: Where was the counter schedule? Why had they not produced one? Would they adopt such a cavalier attitude to the legal requirements of a trial? Again, I came to no conclusion.

On 26 January Fred booked rooms in a London hotel near to the High Court. The hotel had facilities for the disabled. I felt trapped and confused and on 28 January I spent the day in front of my computer composing yet another letter to the solicitor. This letter outlined my views on and questions about the whole affair. I type using one finger of my right hand, the only way to express my thoughts, as I find prolonged, intelligible conversation at an acceptable volume impossible. I had no idea how the 'other side' planned to question me at the trial.

Although the 'other side' had made an additional offer they had failed to pay the money into court. Therefore £1.3 million remained the amount which had to be bettered by the trial. If I was awarded less money, I would be obliged to pay the costs of the trial which would be considerable. The solicitors advice and that of the QC was to make preparations to go to court.

The 'other side' informed me that they refused to accept the witness statements written by my children, my sister and a professional colleague of my husband's. The solicitor asked me to tell these witnesses they would be required to give evidence and face cross-examination at the trial. He would contact them with details of the court, while still trying to obtain the counter schedule.

I used the fax facility on my new computer to send a letter to the solicitor. It had been a difficult letter to compose, as it portrayed my reality, the effects of the injuries I had sustained in the accident, the role of the therapies and the need for care, as I saw it.

On 30 January I heard from the solicitor there was still no counter schedule and the meeting with the QC was postponed once more. In an attempt to obtain the counter schedule the solicitor arranged to serve a court injunction. If no counter schedule appeared, we would understand they had no response to our schedule.

I ended the month, as I had begun it, in deep thought and very anxious. Normally, I do not think about the future, it is a very scary place. Nor do I allow myself to think about how my life has been affected by the accident. The accident had happened. It was up to me to live the rest of my life to the full. I thought the role of insurance was to facilitate this endeavour. Recent events obviously required me to think of the past and contemplate the changes the accident had brought to my future. I was perplexed by the actions of the 'other side'.

CHAPTER XV

13 Crucial Days

Sunday, 1 February 1998
I tried in vain to prepare for the trial. I had no idea about the procedure. Television programmes are usually concerned with criminal activity therefore what little court room knowledge I had was largely irrelevant. I read through all the major reports. Fred was occupied with the same task. I became more concerned as the day wore on and the full extent of the undertaking became clearer. I did not know what the next weeks, days, or even the next hours would bring.

My apprehensions about court procedure paled into insignificance when I considered what going to London and staying in a hotel actually entailed. Since the accident, apart from the extended visits to hospitals, I had remained at home. Problems flashed through my mind: special diet – hemiplegia – dysphagia – medication – double vision – partial deafness in one ear – tinnitus – severe brain injury – ileostomy – the exercise regime – the necessity to sleep on a pressure-relieving air mattress. The longer I thought about it, the more concerned I became.

In an attempt to prevent panic I convinced myself that there must have been similar cases.

Monday, 2 February
I heard from the solicitor – the counter schedule was expected by 4.00 p.m. the following day. The 'other side' had requested two

additional pieces of information. One, I was able to supply – Fred's date of retirement. The other, I was unable to supply because they did not exist – the case manager's notes for an interview with me that predated her employment.

Tuesday, 3 February
I had answers to some of my questions when I saw the counter schedule. The 'other side' finally disclosed the second report written by their medical expert. I was informed by the 'other side' that their experts were rewriting their reports. How or why I did not know, as I had had no communication with their experts. It was the rewritten reports they planned to use in the trial. They had already received the first of the rewritten reports, and sent a copy to my solicitor.

I admit my knowledge of legal procedure is very limited but this rewriting practice was contrary to my understanding of accepted legal procedure. I had already spent many thousands of pounds requesting a number of experts to write reports for me. In addition, I had spent more money requesting the experts I had used to provide comments on reports written for the 'other side'. I had a date, set by the court, when all reports were to be disclosed, and that date was months before. The very late appearance of the counter schedule, the doctor's August report and the proposed use of rewritten reports confirmed the 'other side's' understanding of the legal process was very different from mine.

A quick glance at the counter schedule provided answers to several more of my questions. The schedule of loss and the counter schedule shared very little common ground. I began to formulate conclusions.

The 'other side' did not accept my witness statements, therefore everybody who had written one for me was required to appear at the High Court at 10.30 a.m. on Monday, 9 February. Six days' time! I was reminded I would be required to pay a large part of the 'other side's costs' if my actions caused an unnecessary trial.

The solicitors for the 'other side' also queried various items on the schedule of loss, saying they could not find the receipts for certain of my expenses. Fred agreed to go through the hundreds of receipts and make copies of the ones in question. They also raised questions about the building costs so that the architect could be made aware of the problematical areas before the trial. Likewise in response to questions raised by the counter schedule, the forensic accountant and the care consultant were asked to check some of their figures. My turmoil continued.

The 'other side' had expressed the wish to question me at the trial. They pointed out, in a letter, that I would require the support of my family. The solicitor was fully aware of the difficulties I faced, difficulties which no amount of family support could alleviate. He decided to raise this problem with the QC at the much postponed pre-trial meeting. This meeting was now arranged for the Friday before the Monday we were due in court. The QC had also received copies of the latest documents.

Wednesday, 4 February
The pressure of the legal activity was playing havoc with my normal routine. Yesterday, I had cancelled going to the Resource Centre. Today, at the end of the physiotherapy session the therapist worked with the carer. He demonstrated exercises designed to help reduce pain and spasticity over the trial period.

Kathryn telephoned to say she planned to travel to London on Sunday night; Kathleen was travelling from Leeds on Saturday and was due to complete her journey to London with us on Sunday evening. We booked two additional rooms in the hotel to provide accommodation for them. Matthew and Fred's colleague were going to travel to London on Monday morning. The expert witnesses had all received subpoenas for the week of the trial. All participants had made arrangements to be away from work for as long as they were needed.

I spent the evening working on a response to the counter schedule. I followed this with a very anxious, sleepless night. When morning approached I had reached several conclusions.

Thursday, 5 February

In an attempt to prepare for tomorrow's meeting with the QC and to confirm my overnight conclusions, I reread all the new documents. Fred took a day's annual leave and we worked together on a response to the counter schedule.

Fred was busy hunting through the filing cabinet to find the receipts. One very tangible result of legal activity is the generation of huge amounts of essential documentation. We used a small filing cabinet to contain it all! Fortunately, Fred and I had academic backgrounds, we are both computer literate and enjoyed easy access to the necessary software, hardware and a photocopier – all were essential. However, we still found the requirements of the legal aspect of the insurance procedure daunting and very time-consuming. I can only imagine how less fortunate people manage – or can they manage, faced with such a barrage of difficulties?

The counter schedule was constructed using the expert opinion of a quantity surveyor of building work, the care consultant and an accountant's report. The opinion of their own medical expert was completely ignored.

The accountant's report only included costing for those items of expenditure considered essential by the care consultant and the quantity surveyor, plus any expenditure for which the 'other side' had provided the receipts. This report clearly indicated he had not seen all the documentation from our experts, and he had not seen all the relevant receipts.

The counter schedule was a response to our schedule of loss, therefore in making the response the 'other side' had a copy of the revised schedule of loss, all of the documents, receipts and reports we had disclosed and their own reports, including the two reports from their own medical expert.

The total sum derived by the counter schedule came to less than the rejected 1996 Christmas offer and considerably less than the 1997 Christmas offer which I had just rejected. My reality and the picture portrayed by the counter schedule could be of two entirely different situations. I was completely baffled. Hence the further sleepless night.

The schedule of loss reflected my reality and the opinion of the full range of expert witnesses I had employed and the opinion of their medical expert. It was constructed using the legal precedent set by the *Wells* v. *Wells* case.

One of my overnight conclusions was that many of the items disputed were relatively small, so I removed the financial effect of these items from the amount I had claimed.

Those remaining were areas of major disagreement: therapies, care, transport, building work and the loss of my salary and pension. These areas appeared in both sections of the schedules i.e. up to the trial and again in the projected future losses. I disputed many of the comments made about the therapies and the care I had received in the past. However a further nocturnal conclusion I had reached was, the past is the past. I also removed their combined financial effect from the amount I had claimed.

The future therapy and care regimes advocated in the counter schedule were presumably derived by a distillation of all the information available to them. I can only guess at the rationale which was used in the construction of the document. The results of this process were that neither hydrotherapy, nor aromatherapy were agreed as reasonable treatments. Physiotherapy was reduced to three sessions per week. I would not require counselling services in the future.

Speech therapy appears to have ended – nil.

The 'other side' arrived at this conclusion despite the comments of their own care consultant.

> I agree with the Speech Therapy report that Mrs Davison would require three monthly reviews with a possibility of four top-up sessions every nine months [The current practice].

I have no idea how the 'other side' decided which expert's opinion to utilize and which to discard. The comments of their own medical expert included:

- one of her major ongoing problems is that of profound spasticity (stiffness) in the left arm and leg and there is no doubt that spasticity can be reduced by constant physiotherapy input. It would be reasonable for this to be on a daily basis even if the duration of the treatment was no more than one hour.
- she has a slurring of speech (dysarthria) and it is both difficult for her to talk and difficult for people to understand her.
- she has profound difficulty with swallowing.
- she has a mixture of both anxiety and depression entirely due to the effects of the accident.

These opinions agreed with those of the expert witnesses we had used and are reflected in current practice.

The opinion of the care consultant in her original report had been:

> Physiotherapy – I would therefore recommend two sessions per week at £25 per session.
>
> Hydrotherapy – unless this is recommended by the consultants I believe this would be an option and should be funded by the Davisons if they require it.

They had received a consultant's report recommending hydrotherapy.

> Massage and Aromatherapy – once again I believe this is a choice

rather than a necessity and it should therefore be funded by the Davisons.

We had disclosed a consultant's reports supporting its use.

The section of the counter schedule dealing with care produced a mixture of feelings in me: disbelief, annoyance, perplexity and amazement at their lack of appreciation of, or sensitivity towards, my situation as I saw it. I can only guess at the reasoning behind their opinion.

> A reasonable regime is of a single residential carer recruited under private contract as proposed on behalf of the Plaintiff herself in the... report of January 1995.

Experience, derived over the next three years, proved the proposed regime did not work. We had disclosed reports to illustrate this point.

> Alternatively such is the reasonable regime upon the retirement of the Plaintiff's husband.

> Further the preference of the Plaintiff and her husband is likely to be to minimise intrusion by others at weekends when he is at home, and upon his retirement.

This sentence showed the 'other side' had no appreciation of reality as I saw it:

> The regime proposed at a cost of £45,180 pa plus case manager is disproportionate to the present or future needs of the Plaintiff.

This figure included costing for: 24-hour cover to be shared by two carers, each working 7 days on, 7 days off (not the 24-hour nursing cover recommended by their own medical expert) including bank holidays; for a carer to be able to accompany me on trips and holidays; the increase in household expenses incurred providing food and accommodation for a residential carer; agency cover for 3 weeks annual leave for each of the carers.

INJURY, REHABILITATION AND INSURANCE

The total care regime proposed in the counter schedule appeared to be:

– single residential carer including uplift for Bank Holidays, and cost of relief for holidays and sickness £15,989 pa.

The additional items which appeared in the schedule of loss, presumably I was supposed to fund. The section dealing with past losses provided more details regarding Fred's role. They had calculated, I know not how, that Fred was required for 20 hours during the week plus 12 hours at the weekend.

£4 per hr reduced to 75% for the non-commercial element and the absence of tax or NI ie 32 hours per week at £3 per hour.

Thirty-two hours in addition to his full-time job.

This calculation was not repeated or costed in the future losses. I could only conclude that in the future his help would be unpaid help. The future losses did not consider what would happen if my husband was unable, or did not wish, to carry out the care.

This arrangement shared some ground with the care regime proposed by their care consultant.

The cost of a residential live in carer would be approximately £50.00 per day for five days, Monday to Friday.

Dr Davison would still be responsible for his wife's care during the weekend.

As this would not be considered professional care I would suggest costing of £3 per hour = £36 per weekend.

2 weeks holiday £1800.00.

This recommendation was ignored for future losses. However, the expert advise of their medical expert was:

She will never be able to return to her previous occupation and it is not feasible for her to obtain any alternative occupation at any time in the future. She will require lifelong home care support.

Following the visit after the ileostomy, his recommendation for care now referred to nursing cover:

> She still requires 24 hour nursing cover.

His comments and our disclosed reports seemed to be ignored.

Transport and the building costs appeared in both sections of the counter schedule. Costing for these categories was also considered in the accountant's rewritten report; my perplexity increased.

There appeared to be a misunderstanding concerning the use I made of taxis. The counter schedule:

> Not agreed. In so far as the plaintiff is entitled to claim the cost of a vehicle, this claim save for isolated instances of necessity duplicates that claim and is unreasonable. Further the costs claimed are unreasonably high; and the cost of travel for hydrotherapy and aromatherapy are not accepted on the basis that the treatment was not reasonably necessary.

The occasions when I used taxis were before the building alterations were complete. We could not employ a residential carer to drive me to the various venues, because we were living in the middle of a building site with my husband supplying much of the care.

I travelled on my own thereby reducing the care costs. I only claimed for the care I actually used. A careful look at the dates would have made this clear. To buy the vehicle earlier, we would have had no driver.

The taxi fares to physiotherapy appeared high because there was not enough time for the driver to leave me during a therapy session and return to collect me at the end of the session. The taxi fares from the Resource Centre reflected mileage and were no higher than the normal rate. The cost of care for the two days would have been considerable. I travelled to the centre by the Readibus, I had no receipts, so I made no claim. I could only assume the 'other side' had no understanding of the situation as I saw it. I am sure

INJURY, REHABILITATION AND INSURANCE

recruitment of a live-in carer into a building site would have been impossible.

The latest rewritten accountant's report contained an elaborate argument concerning the purchase of the Sharan. He concluded I had purchased the top of the range model with all the extras. Even then I would have money to spare.

In reality I had purchased the cheapest basic model. The only extras were ABS and air-conditioning. Extras I considered essential to minimize my tinnitus and for a vehicle used by multiple drivers.

These costs were small compared with the cost of the conversion. The vehicle had to allow easy wheelchair access so the carer could manage on her own. The back of the vehicle had to be altered to enable loading via a ramp. The rear bank of seats had to be removed. One further seat was removed from the middle of the next bank. The floor was lowered at this point to be in line with the loading ramp. The two adjacent seats had to be made smaller, to allow for the width of the wheelchair. The exhaust system and the fuel tank were altered to accommodate this change. I am tall, therefore the roof had to be raised.

We had provided the 'other side' with the receipts for the purchase of the vehicle and the adaptation work. I was surprised their accountant had not been furnished with the facts. I had not been seen by him, therefore he could not appreciate my height.

The counter schedule stated:

> Extra mileage is likely to be modest, the rate per mile itself only 20p or so and the extra cost offset in whole or part by the saving on travel to and from work and the like which the Plaintiff no longer has to fund.

I used to walk to work! But for the accident I would still be enjoying my work. We now live in a rural area and I travel in excess of 200 miles each week to receive the various therapies.

13 CRUCIAL DAYS

This sentence shows little understanding of my reality. Of all the statements in the counter schedule this was the most hurtful.

The section in the counter schedule concerned with the building work revealed yet more discrepancies:

> £52,441 is not related to nor reasonably required by the disability of the Plaintiff.

I have no idea how this figure was derived. Neither I, nor the bungalow, were seen by anybody from the 'other side' concerned with building work for a disabled person. This renders precision – to the exact pound – quite remarkable!

The adaptations were planned and supervised by a team of architects who had specific qualifications for working with disabled people. They saw me to assess the nature of my disabilities and closely followed the alterations.

To deal with my salary and pension was difficult for both sides. In the event the two crystal balls showed very different pictures. Neither I nor anyone else had any way of knowing which was the most accurate vision.

My perplexity was complete when Fred found the receipts – they had already received copies.

Friday, 6 February

In the morning I received a telephone call. I was informed the 'other side' were experiencing some unspecified difficulties and had requested a delay of one day, or at least until lunchtime on Monday. I had asked six witnesses of fact to attend the trial on Monday, but I agreed to delay the proceedings until lunchtime. Shortly afterwards the solicitor was informed my children would not be needed at the trial.

The pre-trial conference with the QC was set for 2.30 p.m. at the solicitor's Reading office; my husband and I attended this meeting. It soon became apparent there were other meetings concerned with the impending trial taking place elsewhere.

During the meeting the QC's clerk telephoned to say there were three cases to be heard at the High Court on Monday, each required category A judges, but only two were available. The other two cases were medical negligence cases and therefore took precedence. I was offered either a less senior judge or a delay until a senior judge was available. The QC thought it was very likely that one of the other two cases would be settled out of court, so he recommended that we agree to wait.

During the pretrial conference we also heard from the 'other side'. The first communication informed me they would not require Fred's colleague to attend the trial. The second was a request for the release of my medical notes from all the hospitals I had attended, plus my GP's notes. It was now late Friday afternoon, the trial was the following week, and the date of the trial had been known for months. I could only guess at the reason for this latest requirement, at this time.

The QC was asked how to deal with the problems raised by my being required for questioning. He was also concerned about me giving evidence in a large room, with a weak voice. He suggested all my recent correspondence should be compiled to form a further witness statement.

He suggested Fred should also write a statement explaining his professional role as leader of a research team, the requirement to be available whenever his work demanded, the necessity to attend international scientific meetings which are usually held abroad. This statement would be used to illustrate one of the difficulties of the care plan proposed in the counter schedule.

We were advised to disclose both statements to the 'other side' in advance of the trial. They would also be used during the trial.

After the meeting we contacted the people directly affected by the events of the meeting. I wrote in my diary:

I cannot take much more.

It was fortunate I did not know that events were set to become a lot more complicated.

I had other issues demanding my attention. The district nurse called at the bungalow, as she had arranged for a chiropodist to see me. She hoped he would be able to provide a solution to the ongoing problems with my inflamed big toe.

Later that evening my computer received its first fax – a compilation of my recent correspondence.

Saturday, 7 February
A day of much thought and little activity save that of the visit of the chiropodist and the collection of Kathleen from the railway station.

Sunday, 8 February
A long hard day, Fred and I both worked on the final version of the statements. We sent copies, by fax, to the solicitor's office. I went to bed extremely stiff and my left side was very painful but I consoled myself with this thought: I had done everything I could to make the other side aware of my reality, the need for 24-hour care and all the therapies.

Monday, 9 February
The day began with an early telephone call from the solicitor. He explained he was going to London to work with the QC to prepare for the trial, which he thought would begin on Tuesday, 10 February. Both of the statements were being typed and would be disclosed later that morning.

The solicitor's secretary telephoned, she was trying to fulfil the request made by the 'other side' to see copies of all my medical notes. We were able to tell her the names and addresses of the five hospitals I had attended and the name and address of my GP. She prepared the forms and faxed them to me.

To allow the release of confidential information the forms required my signature. Although I have a computer and a printer I do not have a scanner, therefore I did not have the facility to return signed forms.

Throughout the morning everybody had been involved collecting and packing the items we would require in London. We decided to complete packing the car, start the journey and stop at the post office in order to fax the signed forms to the solicitor's office. Everything was stacked in the hall ready to leave when the telephone rang.

I was told the offer of £1.5 million and an agreement to pay costs had been reinstated. The two additional witness statements had made no difference to the amount offered. As usual there was additional pressure and a decision was required by 4.30 p.m. I was told the money would be placed in court therefore £1.5 million was now a formal offer.

I needed legal advice. I thought I could not speak to a QC without my solicitor being present, the solicitor would not be available until 3.30 p.m. and then only on his mobile telephone. Of course, he was in London with the QC preparing for the trial. We decided to delay the journey until I had spoken with the solicitor.

My mind ranged over the activities of the last eighteen months. My reality underpinned the schedule of loss. The 'other side's' perception of my reality underpinned the counter schedule. It was of little surprise to find major disparity between the two documents. These two documents would go to the judge at the trial.

The events of the last weeks and the offers made by the 'other side' had altered my perception of the whole affair. I had initially thought there was a quest by both sides to establish reality. Events leading up to the first offer of one million pounds had shown this was not the case. I then thought the latest schedule and counter schedule were important. Together they would be used to decide the size of the settlement. The most recent events indicated I needed to change my thinking again.

What would the court be able to use to decide the size of the settlement? I concluded, rightly or wrongly, I was involved in a 'game'. I likened this 'game' to a sport which needed a pitch, rules and a bat. Experience playing the 'game' would obviously help. Although I was unaware, I had been playing the 'game' for some time. What other explanation of the facts could there be? The claim, contrary to all records and available evidence, that I wasn't wearing a seat belt. The Christmas offers – manoeuvres. The preoccupation with my sell-by date. The direct approach, by the insurance company, to one of their experts for her opinion on a range of subjects upon which she was not qualified to comment. The late disclosure of their own medical experts report and their complete disregard of his expert qualified opinion. The very late request to see my medical notes. The debate concerning liability. The use of deadlines. The proposed plan to tell the judge about the offers. Requiring a court injunction to obtain the counter schedule. Rewriting all their reports to use in court. Requiring me to give evidence at the trial. Withholding relevant documentation from their experts. An expert's report on building works for a disabled person written by someone who had no experience building for people with disability. Now requiring a decision by 4.30 p.m., when my legal advisers were in London – when the trial should have started.

I could only assume they would carry on playing the 'game'. Their behaviour indicated to me they had a cavalier attitude towards rules of procedure as I understood them. They had more experience playing the 'game'; I had never considered the process to be a game, it certainly wasn't to me.

They must have been to this point and beyond many times

before, and were able to use their experience to make sure the case they prepared, the bat, was the correct one for the pitch. I had no experience of the 'game' – would my case, my bat, be the right one for the pitch? Could I take the risk? What would happen if the 'game' was tennis and required a nine hundred thousand pound racquet and I had fashioned a two million pound cricket bat?

I rather belatedly thought I understood the reasoning behind the 'game' and its need for the different rules of procedure. I lost my innocent naivete.

I reminded myself of what I had been told would form the basis of a settlement. These were: what the judge believed was the correct version of the schedule of loss, plus an amount for the pain and suffering caused by the accident and a sum to cover the interest on the total settlement since the case was first set down.

If my actions were interpreted by the judge to be those that brought about an unnecessary trial I would have to pay costs, which could be a considerable amount.

What was important to me? I had already decided to only concern myself with future losses for care and therapies. My career had gone and had no part to play in my future. Pain and suffering – hopefully the worst was over. I had a large daily dose of medication to control the remaining pain. Interest on the settlement since the case was first set down – what I had never had, I would not miss. I removed the combined financial effect of all the items from the amount I had claimed.

I recalled the list of questions and attempted to find an answer.

Would I be able to pay for the care? Yes, I thought so, but not the 24-hour nursing cover recommended by their own medical expert, nor the complete range of care outlined in my revised schedule of loss.

Would I be able to pay for the full range of therapies? Yes.

Was my life to consist of pain, care, therapies and nothing else? It would seem so.

13 CRUCIAL DAYS

What obligations did the insurance company have? I had no idea.

What was the status of the schedule of loss, our reports and their reports? They influenced the size of the offers but played no obvious part in the construction of the counter schedule. There was no obvious relationship between the latest offer and the counter schedule. One and a half million pounds and just under nine hundred thousand pounds. This disparity confirmed what I thought I understood to be the rationale behind the 'game'. A game I thought I could not win, I could not afford to lose; I was using a different set of rules and I was exhausted and frightened.

Would the insurance company persistently ignore their own medical expert's reports? Yes, it would appear so.

Would the insurance company carry on believing reports written by people who had neither seen me nor the accommodation? Yes, it would appear so.

Would the insurance company carry on believing the care report? Yes, it would appear so.

Would the insurance company base their offer on her opinion? No, but her opinion would be used in constructing the counter schedule and had a major part to play in the 'game'.

Would the insurance company have a cavalier attitude to the legal requirements of a trial? I had no idea, could I afford to find out?

If the total settlement was less than £1.5 million I would have to pay additional costs from a smaller settlement than was now on offer. If the judge was more convinced by the vision the 'other side' presented in their counter schedule this could easily happen.

The offer was large enough to pay for the various therapies and some care. Had I any right to expect any more? I had to be sure the money offered would meet my future needs so I rang my solicitor's office. He was not there.

The solicitor rang me from his mobile telephone to discuss the situation. He was travelling on a busy train returning to Reading, conversation was impossible. The train was due into Reading at 4.15 p.m., he advised me to speak to him then. Yet more time for thought.

I had moved to live in the bungalow, amongst the building work, to avoid what appeared to be a game of monopoly. Then the stake had been hundreds of thousands of pounds. Now the stake was much larger. On both occasions the amounts were beyond my experience.

The train was now approaching Reading. It was 4.15 p.m., fifteen minutes before the deadline. If I was going to go to court we had to move our cases from the hall and into the vehicle and make our way to London. I could fight no longer, I could not take the risk the court appearance offered. I thought, I understood the 'game' I had no wish to play.

The phone rang. I told the solicitor I had decided to accept the offer. My perception of reality was the only one of any importance. I had to hope the settlement would allow me to manage independently. Only time would tell. I picked up the remaining balls and continued to juggle, unaware that I had stepped on the descending escalator!

Friday, 13 February
Today marks, for me, the beginning of the public phase of the story. I received a note from a friend expressing relief the case was over. How did she know? Several telephone calls later I acquired yet more legal knowledge.

I had given no thought to the requirements of the legal process once I made the decision to accept the offer. I was unaware that the QC would be required to go before the judge and explain the outcome. Equally, I had no idea there would be a press release to the Reading and Cambridge newspapers. Both happened. Under the headline:

13 CRUCIAL DAYS

Woman gets £1.5m as driver accepts blame

London A St Ives man has admitted liability for an accident which led to a £1.5 million compensation deal for a woman left 'dreadfully' injured. Molly Davison, 52, sustained severe head and other injuries... She was a passenger in a car...

The High Court in London heard that despite her injuries Mrs Davison from Reading retained a very active and lively mind.

The court was told that she had been left paralysed down the left side of her body, her mobility was severely restricted and that the accident had had a 'devastating' impact on all aspects of her life.

Her counsel... QC, said her injuries were so grave that it was at first thought she would be legally classified as being incapable of managing her own affairs.

But he told Mr Justice... 'it turns out she has a very active and lively mind. That part of her was mercifully spared the terrible effects of the accident.'

Mrs Davison has sued car driver... who admitted liability. His insurers will also pay her legal costs.

The blanks contain the names of the people involved; it is their actions, not their identity, which are important.

CHAPTER XVI

April 1998 - March 1999

I thought my acceptance of the sum offered concluded the proceedings, but I was wrong.

The settlement, issued from Reading on 6 April read:

> It is ordered that the Plaintiff be at liberty to enter judgment against the Defendant for the sum of £1,144,981.25 inclusive of interest with costs to be taxed if not agreed.
>
> And it is further ordered that the sum of £934,407.20 now in court standing to the credit of this action together with any interest accrued thereon from the date hereof be paid out to the Plaintiff's solicitors, such sum being in part satisfaction of the judgment debt and costs herein and that interest up to the date hereof be paid out to the Defendant's solicitors.
>
> And it is further ordered that the balance of the judgment debt namely £210,574.05 be paid within 14 days of the date hereof.
>
> Dated the 10th day of February 1998.

I learned, for the first time, that the full settlement had never been placed in court and that there was no agreement to pay costs. Against a backdrop of world economic gloom and the reversal by the House of Lords of the *Wells* v. *Wells* settlement, the struggle continued.

As £1,500,000.00 was the total sum awarded, this amount included all the interim settlements, although these interim payments did not reflect what I had actually spent. Was this also part of the 'game'? A further deduction of £31,967.43 was made to cover the amount I owed to the Compensation Reclaims Unit. Therefore, the award became £1,144,981.25 of which £934,407.20 was held by the court. Technically, as far as the court case was concerned, the full amount was in court, although it actually wasn't!

The £934,407.20 together with the interest earned since the settlement became £943,674.43, which was paid in full on 21 April 1998. The rise of £9,267.23 in less than three months, gave me my first indication of the interest the 'other side' had received.

The sum remaining had not been paid into the court, therefore £210,574.05 plus the interest earned since the settlement, should have been paid within 14 days. My solicitor received a cheque on 8 May which failed to reach the amount owed. The solicitor made a deduction of £50,000 to pay a large part of his bill. I was owed £2,440.48 by the insurance company.

The costs of the case were £110,583.67, although this amount was contested by the 'other side'. On 30 June the next battle commenced. The insurance company offered to pay a reduction in the bill of up to 50 per cent, which was rejected. I was advised to pay a taxation fee and to employ a costing clerk to present my case at the taxation hearing.

I rejected several further offers, the last offer being £97,000 plus some interest. There was a taxation hearing on 11 December. The insurance company was ordered to pay £98,188.14, the taxing fee and all the interest that would have been earned on this sum from the date of the trial. I was responsible for the costs I incurred during the taxation procedure.

The case had been settled out of court therefore the bill of costs was considered to be too high. I had already paid, in full, all the medical and legal fees that made up the bill of costs. I did not and do not think they were subject to negotiation or barter. My own solicitor's bill was not considered a part of the bill of costs; I was responsible for the payment of this bill.

INJURY, REHABILITATION AND INSURANCE

Over the following months I received a series of cheques. The trial had concluded thirteen months before and still the legal saga dragged on. At the time of the settlement I had considered the actions of the 'other side' constituted a 'game.' I had now come to realize I was a victim, probably one of many, of a calculated plot that had little regard for my reality or my understanding of legal procedure. When I agreed to the settlement I was guilty of placing the wrong emphasis on the list of questions I had asked myself. The only one of any real importance I failed to answer was: What obligations did the insurance company have?

I accepted the offered settlement because I was ill, frightened, exhausted and trapped. I wanted peace and an end to the battle. The continuing actions of the insurance company denied me that peace as the battle continued.

During an appointment with my solicitor, he explained the legal situation. I had sued the driver of the car, who had paid his insurance premium; in return for this payment he understood the insurance company would meet his legal costs. This was the insurance company's obligation.

If they continued not to honour this obligation, I had two choices: either to forget about the money still owed or to call in the bailiffs. The bailiffs would obtain the money from the person I had sued – the driver of the car, whose mother was a friend of mine.

I had a court order stating I was entitled to the additional money. I instructed my solicitor to pursue the money. I received a further cheque but I was still owed about £2,500. I reasoned the money was mine to use not theirs to withhold. Fred rang my friend to obtain her son's present address. Several days later the insurance company paid the additional amount.

The pursuit of the money proved to be very expensive. I paid all the legal costs I had incurred during the pursuit and the cost of the taxation process. The costs were greater than the money I was owed, a further aspect of the 'game'? I also paid my solicitors' bill for their work to organize litigation and I paid the full costs of the case. I had been warned litigation is expensive!

Compiling the data for this book has obviously had a profound effect on me. Rereading the diaries was very painful; rereading the legal documents very instructive.

> For the purposes of this action and not otherwise the Defendant admits his liability to pay damages for injuries, loss and damage as the Plaintiff may prove to have resulted from the collision complained of in the Particulars of Claim.
>
> The extent of the alleged injuries, loss and damage claimed is not admitted and the Plaintiff is put to proof thereof.

I did prove the extent of the alleged injuries, loss and damage and their own medical expert provided further proof. The driver admitted his liability. All these facts seemed to be ignored by the 'other side'. The medical expert's reports, which should have been used to produce the counter schedule, were ignored. The situation portrayed by the counter schedule was fiction; the dichotomous approach adopted by the 'other side', to my mind, provides confirmation that the 'other side' knew this to be the case. Their tactics ensured that this expert's final report and recommendations played no part in the proceedings; it was disclosed too late.

This whole experience has destroyed many things for me, including my perception of the legal profession and the role of insurance. The accident happened almost six year ago. I have had plenty of time to think but I have not been able to find answers to many of my questions.

If, as an experienced examiner, I had been required to assess the reports used to prepare the counter schedule of loss they would have scored very little. The care report is riddled with factual and fundamental errors, contains unsubstantiated opinion and contradicts both the facts and the opinion of a range of better-

INJURY, REHABILITATION AND INSURANCE

qualified experts. Furthermore the insurance company had requested and subsequently used this opinion. The report concerned with building work for the disabled was compiled without seeing me or the property. The accountant's reports were based on these two reports. He was obviously not shown either the relevant receipts or all the reports we had disclosed.

Why were these documents produced and why were they taken seriously? The counter schedule of loss relies on these documents, so why was it produced and why was it taken seriously? Why can accepted rules of procedure be replaced with tactics? The role of litigation should be to provide financial support for the real situation and to compensate for pain, injury and loss.

The true situation was presented in the medical expert's ignored reports and in my reports. I do need all the therapies and I do need 24-hour care. My life has become a daily quest to try to acquire the necessary professional therapies. Fred does have to provide much of the care. The carers and Fred have to provide much of the extra physiotherapy. I am trapped in an impossible situation, one I cannot influence. I have found other things to influence but that's another story. I refuse to contemplate the future.

Did I receive, as the newspaper said, £1.5 million compensation and an agreement to pay costs, or did I actually receive the financial support for a career change imposed by the accident? A new career, which entails daily exercise, daily pain, no retirement date, no holidays, no weekends, only a sell-by date and the minimum amount of care?

I began writing when I was readmitted into the rehabilitation unit for intensive physiotherapy. I obviously had no idea what the next years would bring. They brought much including, as I had predicted, my metamorphosis.

The driver was careless. What driver can honestly say he or she has never made a mistake? In his case the consequences for me were dire. He was insured, he admitted his mistake and pleaded guilty to careless driving. Consequently, he was fined and received points on his licence. His mistake was neither planned nor premeditated.

The action of the insurance company, in my case, had the power to affect both the process and the outcome of this change. Their response was certainly both carefully planned and premeditated. Maybe in court the true situation would have emerged. I will never know. All their actions must be legal, their behaviour seemed to be that expected from an insurance company. I made the irrevocable decision – did they meet their obligation?